CONTENTS

ACKNOWLEDGEMENTS

The two research projects reported in *Hardship Britain* owe the greatest debt to the many claimants who agreed to be interviewed at length about what were often intimate and painful situations.

The book has also benefited considerably from editorial work by Fran Bennett, Julia Lewis, Richard Kennedy, and from helpful comments made by Saul Becker, Fran Bennett and John Lyons.

Bradford University's Social Fund Project is especially grateful to Goulshan Malik for her help with the interviewing, and also for her general support. We also owe thanks for the advice, help and interest given us by advice workers in the areas where we interviewed, and to local community leaders and imams. We are grateful to Ruth Lister for her support, and also, in particular, to the trustees and staff of the Joseph Rowntree Charitable Trust and the Nuffield Foundation, which provided financial assistance.

The *Family Service Units' Family Poverty Research Project* also wishes to thank the Nuffield Foundation for funding the project, and the Joseph Rowntree Charitable Trust for its additional grant. We are grateful to the members of the Project's advisory group for their support, especially to Jane Ritchie. Finally, many thanks to FSU staff: especially Adah Kay and Mary Hodgson at the London National Office, and individual workers and organisers in the local FSUs where we interviewed.

HARDSHIP BRITAIN

BRITAIN

BEING POOR IN THE 1990S

- Ruth Cohen
- Jill Coxall
- Gary Craig

CPAG Ltd • 1-5 Bath Street • London

CPAG promotes action for the relief, directly or indirectly, of poverty among children and families with children. We work to ensure that those on low incomes get their full entitlements to welfare benefits. In our campaigning and information work we seek to improve benefits and policies for low-income families, in order to eradicate the injustice of poverty. If you are not already supporting us, please consider making a donation, or ask for details of our membership schemes and publications.

This book is published in association with Family Service Units, a long-established charity working with families and children in poor neighbourhoods through 22 units in large towns in England and Scotland, offering a range of social and community work services.

Published by CPAG Ltd, 1-5 Bath Street, London EC1V 9PY

© CPAG Ltd 1992

ISBN 0 946744 37 8

Poverty Publication 82

Cover and design by Devious Designs, 0742-755634
Cover photographs by Mark Power/Network (left), Maggie Murray/Format (right)
Typeset by Boldface Typesetters, 071-253 2014
Printed by Blackmore Press, 0747-53034

FOREWORD

Hardship Britain follows in a long tradition of reports, published by the Child Poverty Action Group, which have attempted to bring home to politicians, civil servants and the wider public the reality of life – or existence, as it is so often experienced and described by claimants – on the social assistance safety net.

At the start of the 1970s, the Group published a study by Virginia Bottomley of a number of East London families living in poverty.[1] A decade later, it collaborated with the Family Service Units (FSU) in producing *Living from Hand to Mouth*, an account of the difficulties faced by 65 families on supplementary benefit and in contact with FSU.[2]

Since this last study was carried out, there have been two major reforms of the social assistance scheme. *Hardship Britain*, which also draws, in part, on research carried out by FSU, represents the most detailed account hitherto of living standards under the post-1988 benefits regime. It builds on and confirms the findings of smaller studies carried out by other charities.[3]

One of the aims of the 1988 reforms was to target help more effectively on low-income families with children. As Jonathan Bradshaw observed in his National Children's Bureau report for UNICEF:

> Over two million children have become dependent on income support and there has been anxiety that the level of benefit, especially for families with children, is not adequate. This was recognised by the Government in its intention to concentrate extra help on families with children in its 1986 White Paper on social security reform. It is not at all certain that this objective was achieved in practice and certainly no attempt was made to define adequacy.[4]

The evidence from the research carried out by Bradford University and FSU, described in this report, suggests that this objective certainly has not been achieved. Moreover, many families are finding it even more difficult to manage now than they did on supplementary benefit. The introduction of the family premium and some modest improvements in children's rates have not been sufficient to counteract the impact of other changes, such as the social fund and the requirement that claimants must meet the cost of water charges and 20 per cent of their poll tax out of their basic benefit.[5] It is hardly surprising that the research reveals 'worryingly high levels of unmet need'.

As well as the general problems of managing on benefit, it highlights the specific problems where there was ill-health in the family. The prevalence of ill-health and disability was marked. Often claimants were getting no extra help from the income support scheme to help them meet the additional expenses caused by disability or ill-health. As a result, they were unable to meet these expenses, thereby aggravating their condition. It would appear that the replacement of supplementary benefit by income support has been particularly damaging to this group of claimants. This is one aspect of the new scheme which needs to be investigated further.

In many cases, parents attributed health problems to the stress of trying to manage on an inadequate income. As an earlier study, published by a local CPAG branch, indicated, it is women who tend to absorb the stress of living in poverty.[6]

The research also points to other psychological effects of living in poverty – feelings of powerlessness, loss of self-esteem, a sense of guilt and stigma. Those on the Right, who argue for the reintroduction of stigma as an explicit tool of social policy, choose to ignore the extent to which the poor already feel stigmatised.[7] As the study found, many prefer to disown the label [of poverty] 'poor' as a result.[8]

Such feelings of stigma have been reinforced in recent years by the growing currency of the language of the 'dependency culture'. Another of the aims of the 1988 and subsequent benefit reforms has been to reduce the dependency on social security and enhance independence. This and other research suggests that the two are not necessarily synonymous. Restrictive social security policies are not the way to make families more independent and total independence is, in any case, a chimera. Such policies simply drive dependency underground into the private sphere, at great cost – emotional as well as financial – to the families concerned.

These costs were felt particularly keenly by parents in the study who felt that lack of money was preventing them from fulfilling their role as parents adequately. Another recent study of benefit recipients similarly noted that 'some of the angriest reactions . . . were from parents who at some stage had felt the state was reneging upon its responsibility to underwrite their own dependability as parents.'[9]

In his Foreword to the *Citizen's Charter*, John Major wrote:

> The Citizen's Charter is about giving more power to the citizen. But citizenship is about our responsibilities – as parents, for example, or as neighbours – as well as our entitlements.[10]

There is accumulating evidence that, by reducing poor citizens' entitlements, the Government has eroded their ability to fulfil their obligations as parents, as citizens.

Poverty is corrosive of citizenship.[11] For women and members of black and minority ethnic communities living in poverty, the exclusion from full citizenship is often compounded. This study contributes to the growing literature which underlines the gendered nature of poverty. This needs to be recognised more explicitly in policy and women's economic position needs to be strengthened. In strengthening women's economic position, we would also be strengthening that of children.

The study also begins to break down the ethnocentric nature of most of the poverty research conducted in this country by looking specifically at the experiences of claimants of Asian origin.[12] This group has been particularly ill-served by the introduction of the social fund. The need for further research in this area is also underlined.

The report concludes with a plea that the views of those who live their poverty, rather than simply research it, should be listened to. It is an appropriate plea at the time of a General Election, the outcome of which is likely to help determine the nature of our society as we move towards the 21st century.

The evidence presented in *Living from Hand to Mouth* just over a decade ago helped to deflect Treasury attempts to cut the real value of supplementary benefit. I hope that the publication of this report will help to ensure that the new government puts poverty at the top of its policy agenda. The needs of those in poverty have been marginalised economically and politically for too long. The voices of those in poverty need to be heard now.

Ruth Lister
Professor of Applied Social Studies, University of Bradford.
February 1992

REFERENCES

1 V. Bottomley, *Families with low incomes in London*, CPAG, 1971.
2 L. Burghes, *Living from Hand to Mouth*, FSU/CPAG, 1980.
3. See eg G.Craig and C. Glendinning, *Missing the Target*, Barnardo's, 1990; R. Smith, *Under the Breadline*, The Children's Society, 1990.
4 J. Bradshaw, *Child Poverty and Deprivation in the UK*, National Children's Bureau, 1990, p25.
5 The 20 per cent requirement will be removed when the council tax replaces the poll tax.
6 Supplementary Benefits Commission, *Low Incomes*, Evidence to the Royal Commission on the Distribution of Income and Wealth, HMSO, 1977, p28.
7 At the benefit rates introduced in April 1992.
8 J. Bradshaw and H. Holmes, *Living on the Edge*, Tyneside CPAG, 1989.
9 See D. Green, 'Foreword' to C. Murray, *The Emerging British Underclass*, IEA Health and Welfare Unit, 1990.
10 For further discussion of this, see R. Lister and P. Beresford, *Working Together Against Poverty*, Open Services Project/Bradford University, 1991.
11 H. Dean, 'Dependency culture: the image and reality of the claiming experience', paper presented to Social Policy Association Conference, Nottingham, July 1991.
12 J. Major,Foreword, *Citizen's Charter*, HMSO, 1991.
13 See R. Lister, *The Exclusive Society: Citizenship and the Poor*, CPAG Ltd, 1990.
14 See also A. Sadiq-Sangster, *Life on Income Support: An Asian Experience*, FSU, 1991.

Hardship
Britain

Poverty is not only about shortage of money. It is about rights and relationships; about how people are treated and how they regard themselves; about powerlessness, exclusion and loss of dignity. Yet the lack of an adequate income is at its heart.

Faith in the City, Church House, 1985

It was in 1989 that the then Secretary of State for Social Security, John Moore, proclaimed 'the end of the line for poverty' in this country. It was also in 1989 that the authors of this book began to prepare the two studies reported here.

The major changes in the social security system introduced a year before, in April 1988, had been hailed by the government as the most significant reforms to the benefits system since Beveridge. The official figures on potential gainers and losers were, however, immediately challenged. In the first year or two following the reforms, concern grew that large numbers of claimants were in reality in a worse financial position than before. But 'transitional protection' had been given to protect the losers' cash incomes (though not their real level); and there was a lengthy 'hand-over' period, in which outstanding claims for one-off single payments tided some claimants over. However, many claimants seemed less than eager to use the new mechanism of the social fund, with its preponderance of loans and its cash-limited discretionary framework.

Now that the new benefit system has been operating for a few years, the picture is clearer. The real impact of rising levels of water rates and the 20 per cent contribution to the poll tax – which from April 1988 had to be met out of benefit – can more easily be seen, and has caused significant problems for many claimants. The radical new system of premiums, with its levelling out of extra payments across broad client groups, can be evaluated. And, now that the social fund, the most contentious part of the reforms (apart, perhaps, from the changes to the state earnings-related pension scheme), has 'bedded down', its inconsistencies and fundamental inadequacies are obvious to all – except, it seems, the government. Refusal rates have only been kept down by injections of extra money several times in each of the last two years. More than one half of all recorded applicants to the main part of the fund are now refused help, and the refusal rate for grants is almost three in four. And some claimants are already on to the twentieth rescheduling of their social fund loans.

Since the research reported in this book was carried out there have also been some changes in government social security policy, and in other relevant policy areas. Some minor real improvements to benefits for some groups of claimants have been made. The level of all poll tax payments was reduced in the 1991 Budget – but the reduction was immediately offset by additional VAT payments. Most importantly, perhaps, unemployment has risen to levels not seen since the early 1980s (and, prior to that, since the 1930s) with its impact spread throughout all regions in the UK and all sectors of employment. As a consequence, many more people find themselves in the situation portrayed in this book than was the case even two years ago – on the receiving end of a benefits system whose inadequacies they have to suffer every day. So it is an appropriate time to publish this, the most detailed independent research to date into the living standards of income support claimants under the post-1988 benefits system.

THE CONTRIBUTION OF THIS BOOK

Debate about the numbers of people in poverty, definitions of poverty thresholds, and comparisons across different claimant groups and between different countries, is critical to the development of effective social policy. This book forms a contribution to this debate, and is expressed, as far as is possible, in the words of poor people themselves. How these people were contacted and the approach used to interview them is described at greater length in the Appendix. In summary, the book reflects the experience of almost 140 income support claimants interviewed in depth (some of them twice) in a number of cities in 1989 and 1990 – ie, one to two years after April 1988, when the 1986 Social Security Act's reforms became operational. As such, it is the first major in-depth study of the experience of income support claimants since the 1988 changes. The research was drawn from two separate and independently organised studies – one by researchers at Bradford University, the other by the Family Service Units (FSU).

From the accounts in the following chapters, readers will be able to draw their own conclusions as to whether the views expressed by those in poverty suggest things have improved since the 1970s when Virginia Bottomley (then a researcher for CPAG) concluded that 'those on supplementary benefit had to make superhuman efforts to budget wisely in the face of increasing pressure on their incomes.'

At the very least, studies such as these preclude the necessity for those who make policy to have to imagine the role that money plays in determining the lifestyles and decisions of poor people. Ironically, one of the strong impressions gained by the researchers was of the reluctance of many claimants to use the words 'poor' or 'in poverty' when applied to themselves, because of the stigma that they felt such terms implied. However, whatever words claimants chose to use to describe their situation, the gap between their needs and the resources offered them by the state was considerable.

POVERTY RESEARCH

There has been a long tradition of research into poverty in the UK, which has attempted to describe the nature of poverty, analyse its causes and effects, and define some kind of 'poverty line' against which society could judge whether differing household types were living in poverty. Such work has grown enormously since the late 1950s and early 1960s, the period when the UK was said to have 'rediscovered' poverty as a result of a number of influential reports.[1]

The thrust of the 1950s/1960s reports was that poverty was much more widespread than had been imagined (or reflected in official reports), both in scope (ie, the number of people in poverty) and in depth (ie, the extent to which poor people's needs were not met by their resources). Townsend's 1957 report showed, for example, that one-third of retired people had incomes below prescribed national assistance levels and that more than a fifth were not receiving the assistance to which they were entitled. These reports also contributed to the growing sense that 'poverty is a dynamic, not a static concept'.[2] This meant that it was relative over time, and that it had a cultural context – 'people are poverty-stricken when their income, even if adequate for survival, falls markedly behind that of the community.'[3] This cultural context has increasingly incorporated the notion of social exclusion: money is clearly important in establishing a base from which to be able to live, but a study of levels of income alone does not reveal the extent to which poor people may be prevented from participating fully in the life of the community.[4]

Since the early 1960s, a considerable number of other studies of aspects of poverty in the UK have been published, covering the definition, measurement, comparison or description of poverty. In addition, some studies have focused on questions of poverty relating to specific claimant groups or on the impact of poverty on a particular dimension of poor people's lives – such as health or social exclusion. Readers who wish to pursue particular themes are referred to the Bibliography as a starting point for further exploration of many of the issues discussed in this book.

IS ANYONE IN POVERTY?

Despite the plethora of studies, arguments continue between governments and the poverty lobby as to the extent and nature of poverty. The most strongly contested recent government contributions to this debate have been the publication of the *Households Below Average Income* (HBAI) data sets and the annual reports of the Secretary of State for Social Security on the social fund. The shift by government to publishing statistics on incomes related to the average – as opposed to measuring the numbers of those living on or close to the supplementary benefit (now income support) level – has been criticised as 'moving the goalposts' in a long-running debate. In the event, the government's interpretation of the data was found to be faulty (and later accepted as such by the Secretary of State for Social Security), as a result of work commissioned by the House of Commons Social Services Committee from the Institute for Fiscal Studies (IFS).[5] The IFS found that the incomes of the poorest 10 per cent of households had risen *less*, not *more* (as government ministers had frequently boasted) in comparison to the population as a whole. More recent reports suggest that the position of the poorest has deteriorated further in relative terms to the end of the 1980s.[6]

On the other hand, in describing the operation of the state's last resort safety net for the poorest, the Social Fund Annual Reports have insisted that 'the social fund is working well' despite mounting evidence of debt, hardship and a growing gap between the needs presented to the fund and its ability to respond to them. This view could only be generally accepted if one perceived the objective of the fund as containing public expenditure rather than as meeting the defined needs of the poorest claimants.

At the time of writing, more than half of even those claimants who reach the point of submitting a formal application to the main body of the fund are refused any help at all. For already almost 100,000 claimants, this will have been on the grounds that they were 'too poor to help' because they could not repay a social fund loan.

In line with growing moves towards economic and (less certainly) social integration of European states, it is also important to reflect on the European dimension to this debate. For example, recent studies have provided data which enable us to begin to incorporate a European perspective into existing research.[7] This allows us to confront the difficult task of comparing poverty levels and definitions between differing nation states. Regrettably, the government's response to this widening of the debate on UK poverty has been to state that 'this whole concept of a poverty line is regarded by ministers as rather absurd'.[8] The EC itself has accepted a wider view of poverty, establishing a Third Poverty Programme specifically for the 'integration of the excluded':[9]

> the poor shall be taken to mean persons, families and groups whose resources (material, cultural and social) are so limited as to exclude them from the minimum acceptable way of life in the member states in which they live.[10]

Even making some allowance for political hyperbole, John Moore's 'end of poverty' speech was breathtaking in its implicit dismissal of the everyday experience of millions of those claiming basic means-tested benefits. No one seriously doubts that the position of the poor has improved, both in absolute and relative terms, since the Victorian era of which he spoke. However, there is also ample evidence (see Bibliography) that means-tested social security benefits have offered claimants a standard of living which has been variously described as wretched, drab and limited, characterised by debt, ill-health, poor housing, and constrained access to opportunities to participate fully in any meaningful way in the life of the community.

NOTES

1. Townsend, P, (1957), *The Family Life of Old People*, Routledge Kegan Paul, Henley. Cole, D and Utting, J, (1962), *The Economic Circumstances of Old People*, Codicotes, London. Townsend, P, (1962), 'The Meaning of Poverty', *Br J Soc*, Vol. 13, No 3, pp210-227. Abel-Smith, B and Townsend, P, (1965), *The Poor and the Poorest*, Bell and Hyman, London.
2. Townsend, P, (1962), see note 1, p219.
3. Galbraith, J, (1958), *The Affluent Society*, Hamish Hamilton, London, p252.
4. Golding, P, (1986), *Excluding the Poor*, Poverty Pamphlet No 71, CPAG Ltd, London. Lister, R, (1990), *The Exclusive Society*, CPAG Ltd, London.
5. House of Commons, (1990), *Low Income Statistics*, House of Commons Social Services Committee, HC376, HMSO, London.
6. See, for example, Townsend, P, (1991), *The Poor Are Poorer*, SMU, University of Bristol, Bristol.
7. Eurostat, (1990), Rapid Report, *Population and Social Conditions*, 1990/8, Brussels.
8. *Guardian*, 8 April 1991.
9. Commission of the European Communities, (1989).
10. Bull. EC, 12-1984, pt. 2.1.95.

2 Being poor in Britain

'My life is nothing like this, nothing . . . '

Rashid Chaudry

This book is founded on research which was conducted in 1989/90 in the aftermath of far-reaching changes to the social security system fully implemented in 1988. The purpose of this chapter is to provide a flavour of the experience of living on income support in Britain today. However, before doing so, it gives a brief overview of the 1988 changes and their implications for claimants.

The remainder of the chapter then tells the stories of six individuals and families of varying circumstances selected from the people we interviewed for our research projects.

THE SOCIAL SECURITY REFORMS OF 1988

Amongst the changes which affected claimants most were the replacement of supplementary benefit by income support and the introduction of the social fund. Through these and other reforms, the government aimed to achieve a number of objectives. It wanted to discourage claimants from dependence on the state by instituting a benefit system which would 'leave claimants free to manage their own financial affairs' and encourage 'budgeting skill'. It also sought a more efficient 'targeting' of limited resources, to ensure they reached the claimants it defined as being in the most need – families with children, and elderly and disabled people. Three aspects of the new system were especially important for our research.

Firstly, the introduction of flat-rate additional weekly 'premiums' for parents, pensioners and people with disabilities, which replaced the extra allowances previously granted for special needs – eg, a medically-required special diet, extra heating costs or extra laundry costs. This premium system was considered administratively simpler and a means of targeting extra help on the most needy groups.

Secondly, under the new income support system, claimants were also required for the first time to cover 20 per cent of their general rates (subsequently poll tax) and all of their water rates from their weekly benefit. Formerly, they had not had to pay any rates, and whatever they paid in water rates had been added to their weekly benefit. It was argued that if claimants had to contribute to rates, even the poorest would have an interest in how their local authority fixed its expenditure. A notional amount of £1.30 per week was therefore added to income support benefit levels to cover the 20 per cent contribution to rates.

Thirdly, single payment grants for lump-sum expenses, previously allowed to people on supplementary benefit, were replaced by the social fund. The government felt that expenditure on single payments had been increasing too rapidly, and that this meant many claimants had been receiving help who did not really need it. It also argued that, as benefit had risen in real terms prior to the 1988 changes, claimants no longer needed extra money for many of the items previously covered by single payments. In line with the aims of increasing 'independence' and helping people to budget, the social fund would therefore mainly provide repayable loans, with grants only available to relatively few people under limited circumstances. This part of the social fund was cash-limited and discretionary.

THE EFFECTS ON CLAIMANTS

These changes were to have major effects on the weekly budgets of income support claimants. The Bradford and FSU research findings lead us to four major conclusions:

- Benefit levels are far too low to allow claimants to budget effectively – price rises and the requirements to meet part of rates and

all of water rates have not been adequately compensated for;
neither has the removal of most lump-sum grants. The real rises
in income support for some groups, since this research was
carried out, have not been significant enough to reverse this
general judgement.

- Because of this basic inadequacy, the income support plus
  premium system has largely failed as a method of targeting
  resources at the 'needy'. Not only are the 'less needy' – for
  example, young single people – suffering; but also many of those
  defined as 'more needy' – eg, those who are disabled, elderly or
  with children.
- The social security changes have not resulted in a reduction in
  dependency. In many cases, claimants' dependence on state provision has simply been transferred elsewhere – eg, to a reliance on
  family or friends. Where this transfer is not possible, claimants are
  all too often left to go without.
- The difficulties caused to claimants by the inadequacy of benefit
  levels were, in many cases, exacerbated by their experience of the
  administration of the social security system. The income support
  system seemed no simpler in their experience and was often
  perceived as hostile, demeaning or racist.

WORSE OFF SINCE 1988

Most people felt they did not have enough money to provide an
adequate standard of living. Statements like 'it's not enough to
survive on' or 'we just exist' occurred frequently in interviews. A
lone parent summed up the common predicament:

> By the time I've done the shopping, and that doesn't even last a week,
> I'm penniless . . . You never have any money.

What this meant in terms of debt, deprivation and unmet need is
explored in more detail later in the chapter.

Over two-thirds of the people in the Bradford study were quite
explicit that, in financial terms, they were worse off since the 1988
benefit changes. Those entitled to an increase in 1989 received on
average only one or two pounds a week, and pointed out that this
did not cover even the rise in fuel and food prices. The fact that the
3.9 per cent rise in 1989 covered the 'average' inflation rate was of

little comfort, given that gas prices alone rose by eight per cent in 1989. The steep rise in inflation in the second half of the year made the situation worse. Many claimants were clear that benefit increases did not, in practice, compensate for the increased cost of living. In addition, people in both studies complained that they had been affected by the shift from grants to loans.

Over a third of the Bradford claimants had had no benefit increase at all in 1988 or 1989. This was usually because of the way the changeover from supplementary benefit to income support was achieved. Some people had been entitled to more from supplementary benefit than they were due to receive under the new income support rules – most often because they had been allowed extra supplementary benefit for special needs or for claiming long-term. Under these circumstances, benefit was frozen at the old rate until the yearly upratings of income support caught up with it. This was intended to ensure that some claimants did not actually receive an increase with the introduction of income support, but the effect was to leave these people unprotected against inflation.

Paying towards rates and water rates was an additional burden. As we have seen, only £1.30 was built into new weekly benefit rates to cover general rates and no separate amount had been allowed for water rates. Yet in 1989, the Yorkshire region raised their water prices by 15 per cent; Bradford claimants' water-rate payments ranged from £1.75 to £3 per week and general rates contributions from £1.10 to £4 per week in 1989. The FSU study showed claimants paying at a similar level: in 1989 only one person was paying less than £2 for water rates and general rates taken together, while 33 out of the 38 people who could provide figures were paying between £2 and £10.

Any combination of these extra costs caused hardship to claimants, but where all of the factors were present the level of hardship was severe. This was the case with Mr and Mrs Davis, aged 54 and 47, with no dependent children, who had been on benefit for two years when interviewed in September 1989. Mrs Davis was a wool comber but work was intermittent and, in spite of completing a further training course in 1987, she was unable to find work. In addition, Mr Davis had high blood pressure and chronic bronchitis, and Mrs Davis suffered with ulcers and required a special diet.

With the 1988 changeover to income support from supplementary benefit, they were no longer entitled to additional benefit for dietary costs or to the higher long-term rate of benefit. As a result, their benefit was frozen at the £63.50 per week they had received from April 1987. As well as rising fuel bills, they now had to pay rates and water rates totalling over £5 per week with no extra money to compensate. They found paying bills and buying special food increasingly difficult. The worry of unmet bills coupled with a social fund loan repayment (the loan was taken out to cover an outstanding gas bill), combined with a deteriorating diet, took its toll of Mrs Davis' health. At the end of 1988 she was hospitalised, first for depression and then for an ulcer operation.

Although the benefit changes also aimed to target more money at those with dependent children, the families interviewed were little better off than those without children. Forty-two of the 52 families with children interviewed in Bradford stated that they were worse off financially since the changes. Half had had no benefit increase in either 1988 or 1989. Most of those whose benefit did go up said that it was inadequate to cover price rises.

SIX STORIES

Whilst every individual is unique, those whose stories are reported here are reasonably typical of the people we interviewed. Certainly, their circumstances are not especially severe as compared with others. Their stories illustrate the themes to be covered in subsequent chapters, including:

- how difficulties of budgeting on benefit often lead to material hardship – for example, people are regularly cutting back on basics like food and heating because they have inadequate income;
- ill-health is prevalent and lack of money makes it difficult for people to cover health-related expenses;
- despite wanting to change their situation, many people feel trapped and powerless to improve life for themselves and their families. This results in considerable emotional stress;
- lack of money often also leads to exclusion from normal social activities, and this is felt to be particularly hard when it affects children;
- finally, other factors apart from money affect the overall quality of life experienced by poor families – for example, inadequate housing and a lack of local services also have an impact.

STORY ONE:
'I'M JUST STUCK HERE': MRS AUSTIN

Elsie Austin is a 76-year-old disabled widow who has been on supplementary benefit and then income support since 1983. She lives
alone in a council bungalow which is structurally sound, but her
bedroom is very cold. Mrs Austin suffers from hiatus hernia and
deformed feet which make walking very difficult. Because of her
disability she needs a specially-adapted shower, but the local social
services department has refused to provide one. She cannot get out at
all unaided and her only visitors are a mobile hairdresser once a
fortnight and, occasionally, her daughter, who takes her shopping.

When we saw her in 1989, Mrs Austin received £45.26 retirement pension plus £3.34 income support per week. Her benefit only
went up by 50p in 1988 and 30p in 1989; because of this she had to
cut down on her heating and food consumption.

Mrs Austin budgets strictly, calculating her bills to the penny and
putting money away each week. Some weeks she manages to save a
little for Christmas, but she had not been able to save towards a
holiday for 1990. Her last holiday was paid for by a £100 premium bond win. Having to pay rates and water rates has had a big
effect:

> It's nearly £100 a year . . . I could have this to go on holiday.

She uses a mail-order catalogue to buy some clothes and bedding
and is currently paying off a small purchase at £2 per week. She
never uses charity shops or second-hand dealers, preferring to
manage with the clothes she has and furniture which either pre-
dated her retirement or has been provided by relatives.

After a life-time of work and saving, Mrs Austin has most of the
things that she needs for her home in the way of household durables
and furniture. However, her small savings were used to finance the
move to her bungalow and now she has nothing left to fall back on
in an emergency. If she needed to replace anything:

> I'd have to do without paying my gas bills or do without my food if
> the cooker broke down. I'd have to buy a new one on hire purchase
> and pay the instalments by cutting down on food.

This situation obviously makes her feel insecure:

'You worry every week, wondering if you're going to have enough, and what you're going to have to go without.'

You worry every week wondering if you're going to have enough . . . how things are going to go.

POVERTY AND ILL-HEALTH

Mrs Austin's main problems are her poor health and resulting isolation, but these are compounded by poverty. The pain in her feet makes it hard for her to sleep properly. On top of this, she is unable to afford to put the heating on in the bedroom and in the winter this makes it too cold to sleep at night. Such problems are accentuated by the mattress on her bed which is lumpy and uncomfortable, but she cannot afford to get a new one. Mrs Austin finds it more comfortable to get up during the night but:

> I can't have my gas fire on at night . . . it's a bit of a problem if I do this because there's nothing left [money] and there's food to pay for beside this.

Mrs Austin cannot afford to be comfortable in her old age.

BOREDOM AND ISOLATION

Mrs Austin's problems with her feet mean that she cannot get out and about unaided. In addition, alongside this she cannot afford to console herself with 'little luxuries', such as nice food or a video, that others might use in her situation:

> I never go out now . . . never go nowhere. I can't afford sweets . . . don't have any entertainment, all I ever do is watch TV, read and listen to the radio.

She cannot manage the walk to the local bus but used to make use of a special bus service called the Freedom Ride which would pick her up from the house, take her to the shops and then drop her back. This service has been cut by the local council and she now finds it difficult to shop, but a taxi is out of the question:

> I haven't been out this week and there's one or two things I could do with. If I want to get out now I've just got to get a taxi but it costs over £2 now each way so that's nearly £5 on your bill before you've started.

Her relatives live quite a way off, rarely visit, and do not have time to take her out:

> I can't go out now unless my daughter takes me . . . my daughter takes me out now and again but she works you see, she's a receptionist, she's no time now.

The only time Mrs Austin gets out of the house is to go to a pensioners' lunch club at a local school once a week. But it is not just the boredom or the inconvenience that gets her down. She is a lively and friendly woman and the sheer lack of human company and mental stimulation makes her despair. Talking about the special bus service, she explained:

> I used to go shopping for an hour, I used to go to Morrisons [local supermarket], they [helpers] would bring all your parcels into the kitchen for you – they were really lovely with me . . . really lovely.

If she had the money she would take a taxi out to see people as she gets very few visitors:

> At the moment I'm just stuck here. I feel like climbing the walls sometimes – last week I had two days where I never saw a soul . . . nobody came, nobody rang up, they never ring up, I can't get out, I'm stuck here.

Mrs Austin is indignant that she should be so deprived in her old age, and has become quite depressed, seeing little hope for the future:

> We've earned our pensions and now there's nothing to look forward to. I sometimes wish I'd go in my sleep.

STORY TWO:
'NOT ENOUGH TO DO AND NOT ENOUGH TO EAT': THE DOWNINGS

Andrew and Christine Downing, aged 31 and 29, have three small children aged 8, 6 and 2 years and a baby aged 15 months. The family have been on benefit for 10 years. Despite attending various government training schemes, Andrew has found it hard to get a job. He believes this to be the result of his (minor) criminal record. Christine and two of the children suffer from asthma; the youngest daughter has a heart defect and the baby boy has a milk allergy. The family's council house has damp in nearly all the rooms and is hard to heat because of defective windows.

MONEY AND BUDGETING

When interviewed early in 1990, the family received £29 per week child benefit and £64.50 per week income support after deductions for gas, rent arrears and a social fund loan. Andrew signs on and receives his giro weekly. Christine handles the money and, as soon as the giro is cashed, pays £5 per week for general rates (including arrears), £3 for washing machine hire and £10 worth of electricity tokens.

Andrew estimates that, in real terms, they were £9 per week worse off in 1989/90 than they were prior to the 1988 benefit changes. The Downing's benefit has been 'frozen' for two years (no uprating in 1988 or 1989), yet since 1988 they have had to pay water rates and 20 per cent of the general rates (and then poll tax). The family found it impossible to keep up with water rates payments in the first year and were eventually taken to court for non-payment. They are now slowly repaying that year's arrears as well as the second year's water rates at £8 per month. The baby's milk-free diet is an additional burden and their finances are stretched impossibly tight.

Despite careful budgeting, the Downings find that they have to cut down on fresh food and heating in order to save on electricity bills. There is never any money for leisure or entertainment, or even enough to allow for variety in daily consumption.

HEALTH AND COMFORT

In order to economise on heating bills, the family boils kettles rather than using the immersion heater. They also cannot afford proper heating:

> With him [child] being asthmatic we should have the electric heating on in the bedrooms . . . we can't do it which is why he is like he is now [ill] . . . he's chesty all the time.

The Downings are extremely frustrated at not being able to afford to buy a decent vacuum cleaner to tackle the dust which aggravates the children's asthma. Ironically, they could have reduced expenditure on electricity if they could have afforded the £30 needed to unblock the chimney of their wood burner stove, which is much more efficient than the immersion heater.

Getting enough decent clothes and shoes is also a problem. Shoes for four growing children take up any spare money after bills are paid, leaving little or no money at all for the parents to buy clothes and shoes for themselves. When interviewed, Christine had bought nothing for herself for over a year and Andrew explained: 'I've had one new pair of trousers in the last two years . . . a cheap pair.' This situation is not only uncomfortable – they do not have enough winter clothes – but also demoralising:

> How would you feel, having to root round in a second-hand shop for three hours to find a pair of shoes?

OUT IN THE COLD

Not being able to afford the things that most families take for granted has consequences for family relationships and for the Downings' self-esteem as parents. They have to find ways to be able to afford Christmas, but their options are increasingly limited:

> That was a joke . . . for months before, we were doing without stuff just to buy them small toys . . . they didn't get anything really . . . I had an old video, I had to sell it . . . I got £45 for it to buy food.

Mr Downing described the stress caused by seeing the children go without as the worst thing about being on benefit:

> The kids, if they go to town with you . . . they see stuff . . . you feel awful . . . not being able to buy them stuff kids want.

This is aggravated by a sense of exclusion:

> They go to school with their mates who've got these posh £30 frocks . . . We can't afford them.

Such stress can take its toll on family relationships:

> A more and more current thing is arguing with the wife and snapping at the kids.

The strain is made worse by the limitations imposed on parents' activities:

> We don't go out, we don't go anywhere, we can't even afford to go to the pictures once a month.

Mr Downing explained how their lack of financial resources could turn a normal family drama into a crisis; when their TV broke down they had to find someone who would fix it for nothing:

> A simple thing like a telly is essential . . . if you haven't got a telly for them to watch they have you pulling your hair out because you can't ever get away from them for a night out like working people.

Mr Downing sums it all up:

> Imagine spending a year where the best thing you can look forward to is running a Hoover around the living room and washing up . . . You go mad, your grey cells start turning purple. The kids are running round screaming their heads off, you tend to get ratty, the more often you lose your temper it has an effect on you. By not having enough to do and enough to eat . . . I have enough to eat, I mean what everyone would like to eat. I think it does have an effect on your health both physically and psychologically. It depresses you looking at what other people have and what you can't have.

STORY THREE:
'MY LIFE IS NOTHING LIKE THIS, NOTHING . . .': THE CHAUDRYS

Rashid and Shaheen Chaudry are a Pakistani couple in their late twenties, with three young children (one a baby). Rashid was a textile worker until 1986 when he had to give up work because of severe stomach ulcers; he also now suffers from asthma. Rashid feels that these days he could not work in heavy industry but, although he would like to, he has not been able to find any light work. The family has no savings and no income other than their weekly income support. They live in a small terraced house which they were trying to buy. Structurally the house is reasonably sound, but some of the flooring is defective and they are not able to afford to keep it in a satisfactory state of decoration or repair. For example, external and garden walls need repairing.

MONEY AND BUDGETING

When the giro arrives, the family's first priority is to attempt to pay off any outstanding bills. They do not feel that they have enough money to do a 'big shop' or save money by buying in bulk (they do not have a freezer), so they buy a little day by day. By the time the benefit giro arrives, they have usually accumulated debts which they clear at local shops and then get 'little by little' into the red again when the new giro runs out.

Apart from bills at local shops, the Chaudrys feel that most of their money goes on their children and on bigger bills such as gas and electricity. They can never pay these big bills all at once:

> We try to pay them something and then bit by bit finish them.

For smaller bills, the family put all the money they have together and, if there is still not enough, they borrow from friends. They find this humiliating and 'it's bad if you don't have it when they ask for it back'. There is never enough money to put aside for savings. When the weekly money runs out, the Chaudrys only buy 'what is most important'. This means, for example, that for part of the week fresh fruit and meat are cut out of their diet.

The family have no telephone, vacuum cleaner, electric kettle or freezer and their fridge is in poor condition, as are all their other household goods. Although they try to give the children two hot meals a day, and often feel obliged to give them fruit and sweets (even though this stretches their budget), their lifestyle is in all other respects spartan. For example, the Chaudrys do not have a set of warm winter clothes or two pairs of all-weather shoes for everyone; the children get no treats and the family cannot afford to go to visit friends and relatives in other towns. They cannot afford special clothes for Eid and other festivals. The family is constantly 'doing without' in order to avoid falling deeper into debt. Any extra money is spent on basics such as food and other day-to-day necessities, rather than on anything out of the ordinary.

They had thought about approaching the social fund but decided against it:

> It would be an extra burden – I couldn't afford to take on something else like that, I have enough worries already.

Rashid and Shaheen have occasionally used catalogues in the past to buy items like coats, but generally now rely only on their own local shops for credit – they currently owe about £50 (ie, just under half their weekly income). They have never got deeply enough in debt to be threatened with court action, generally because they have gone without rather than overstretching themselves. The recent poll tax and water rates bills caused further worry. The family's poll tax contribution of 20 per cent was £120 a year and the water rates were a further £90 a year, a total of £4 per week extra to be found from their benefit. Unsurprisingly, they do not feel they can afford to buy better furniture, even from second-hand shops.

WORRY AND PRESSURE

Lack of money is a constant worry:

> I just worry about paying the bills . . . I can't think about when the children grow up . . . the worst thing is just not having enough money to pay the bills, buy the food and look after the children. It's too much from hand to mouth.

Although lack of money puts a strain on their relationship, the Chaudrys told us that they make a concerted effort not to argue too much.

The children are another source of pressure, because of their limited family finances:

> I don't like saying no to the children when the ice-cream van comes and they want something even small like sweets – but sometimes you have to.

Quite often the children have to do without fruit and meat, even though the parents put their needs first:

> I have asthma and when I get worried or I'm not warm, I get worse . . . we put on the heaters for the children because you have to, but for ourselves we say no – whatever little we can give is good – but it's difficult.

It is difficult because there is little in the budget that can be 'given', and:

> . . . it's getting more and more difficult to manage as the children get older.

BEING ASIAN AND POOR

The Chaudrys feel that they are reasonably aware of the social security system. However, their English, although 'not bad', does not prevent them from having problems because there are:

> lots and lots of forms to fill in and lots of questions. They ask the same question in so many ways, it gets very confusing . . . so what about those who can't read or write?

They suspect that they may be treated differently because they are Asian:

> No doubt when they take a long time [at the social security office], they see who we are first and get on with other people's cases first.

In terms of his general situation, Rashid does not feel particularly better or worse off than most people in his area of Bradford:

> There are lots of people here who are unemployed so it's bad for a lot of them, especially those with children, that's very difficult . . . the real problem is that they don't give us enough money.

The Chaudrys like their community, which they feel is well-appointed as regards shops and other facilities. However, the constant strain of budgeting on benefit means that they are doing little more than surviving. Rashid's last words expressed poignantly how he felt about their existence:

> My life is nothing like this, nothing . . .

STORY FOUR:
'STANDING ON SAND AND IT'S WASHING AWAY ALL THE TIME': SANDRA COLE

Sandra Cole is in her forties. She has been on benefit since the birth of her third child 15 years ago and she claims for seven of her eight children who are aged between 16 and two. The family lives in a council flat on a small estate in a pleasant suburb of a northern city. Sandra's elderly invalid mother, who needs a great deal of care, lives opposite. Two of the children are asthmatic, while Sandra herself has developed a stress-related viral condition which she attributes to a combination of financial worries and the stress of nursing her mother.

MONEY AND BUDGETING

In 1989, Sandra received benefits totalling £147.80 per week for herself and the seven children. From this she paid £6.11 a week for rates and water rates. Gas and electricity averaged about £5 each per week and she was also paying £5 a week to a catalogue. Sandra has no savings and the children's father contributes maintenance direct to the DSS, so it makes no difference to her weekly income.

Sandra budgets meticulously each week, economising as much as possible and accounting for every penny. She tries to budget for lump sums too, buying Christmas presents from January onwards, saving up school clothing grants and 'robbing Peter to pay Paul' when bills come. She pays fuel bills in several instalments, but to do this the whole family have to tighten their belts. Indeed, when money is short, she – though not the children – will cut back on food: 'I've known me to have three lots of toast in one day: breakfast, lunch and dinner.'

Clothes for the children are a constant anxiety:

> I've just got to the point now that I don't know where to start, just running around in circles wondering who do I buy for first?

Another major headache is maintaining the home – renewing furniture, appliances and decoration. Sandra is depressed about her inability to keep up standards.

She tries hard to avoid any kind of debt, and partly because of this would not consider taking on social fund loans. She prides herself on being a good manager, but finds it increasingly difficult to budget successfully and keep out of debt. She has cut back more and more over the years. She recalls:

> In the winter I always used to give them soup before their main meal. I can't remember which winter it was but I just had to stop, I couldn't afford the soup *and* a meal.

When re-interviewed in 1990, Sandra said that her finances had become even tighter over the last year:

> In the past I've been able to stretch the money but even with the food
> I notice I'm having to cut down . . .

She had recently had to borrow from a friend (something she always tried to avoid) and cut down even more on food expenditure. During the year she had to replace her fridge, reluctantly turning to a catalogue to do so. In addition, she is extremely worried about how she will manage when her cooker, now on its last legs, finally gives out.

LIVING ON INCOME SUPPORT

Sandra feels guilty about being on benefit and is happier that the children's father pays a considerable amount in maintenance to the DSS. At the same time, she feels she should be at home while the children are growing up, but is worried that later on she will be too old to get a job, in spite of her previous office-work experience.

She has little knowledge of the benefit system, and only claimed in the first place when advised to do so by a health visitor, after months of surviving on savings and maintenance. She hates going to the DSS office and generally feels that the system is designed to make you feel guilty:

> It seems the assumption is that if people are comfortable on the money you're giving them they're not going to make an effort to get any better.

RESTRICTED SOCIAL LIFE

Although she sees friends, Sandra almost never goes out at night except to the occasional meeting. In the past, she was both involved with the church and active in the tenants' association and parent-teacher association. However, in recent times she has had to cut down, partly because she literally lacks clothes in good enough condition for her to feel comfortable attending the meetings. In addition, the family have not been to church for some time because of the expense of collection money for all seven children: 'It just chips away at your self-esteem the whole time.'

Sandra has consciously tried to help the children adapt to lack of money. She puts a great deal of effort into encouraging them with school work, and into providing a warm and supportive family environment. They spend a lot of time together at home and she tries to create enjoyable cheap or free local outings, but this is becoming increasingly difficult:

> We used to go swimming once a week as a family, now we can't do that.

She is aware, though, that it is difficult for them when their friends go out, while a lack of funds ties them to the house.

HEALTH AND PERSONAL STRESS

Because of lack of money, Sandra cannot keep up the standards she sets for herself and the children. She says she likes to be in control and describes how, in her situation, 'you feel like life's doing things to you, you're not in control of life'. All her energies are focused on being a good parent and her inability to provide for the children as she would wish leaves her oppressed by anxiety and guilt.

All in all, Sandra feels under relentless and continuous pressure. After years of struggle her health is beginning to give way. She finds it more and more difficult to cope with the unequal battle to control her finances:

> It's this feeling of never getting on your feet. It's like standing on sand and it's washing away all the time.

STORY FIVE:
'COME WEEKEND AND THE HAND IS EMPTY AS EMPTY': ANJUM ABBAS

Anjum Abbas is in her late thirties. She is separated from her husband and has two sons aged 7 and 12. She has been claiming benefit for six years and is an owner-occupier in a run-down inner-city area.

MIKE ABRAHAMS/NETWORK

'We can't afford good food for the children without taking money from what we've saved for the heating bill, so then we can't put the heating on even though my youngest's got bad chest complaints.'

MONEY AND BUDGETING

In 1989, Anjum received a total of £74.50 income support and child benefit per week. From this she had to pay her mortgage of £75 per month, and rates and water rates totalling £165 per year. She also paid about £40 per quarter for gas and a relatively small amount for electricity. In fact her income support was wrongly calculated so she was effectively meeting the full mortgage payment out of the benefit allowed for the daily needs of herself and her two sons, without the extra to which she was entitled for mortgage interest. Not surprisingly, Anjum found this desperately hard. By 1990, the benefit had gone up by £14 per week because the DSS had apparently started paying the mortgage interest.

Each week Anjum's first priority is keeping up with the mortgage, rates and other bills. Then come TV licence stamps which are important because of the children. Food comes next and then, if possible, children's clothes. She economises stringently on food:

> Whatever runs out first I buy that first and then if there's any money left, which there usually isn't, I can buy other things.

Her money has often run out by the end of the week and she may have to borrow from neighbours or obtain credit from local shopkeepers. She cuts back on her own food:

> Many times I've been without food myself, many times . . . and probably will have to do so in the future, goodness knows how many times.

When money is really tight she simply keeps the children at home and the family live on basics, usually dhal (lentils) and roti (unleavened bread).

In 1989, Anjum borrowed £500 privately from a friend for essential repairs to the bathroom, and to pay off mortgage arrears. She is very worried about how to pay this back: 'Honestly sometimes I can't sleep at night for thinking about it'. By 1990 she had paid some off and borrowed more from another friend to pay the rest. However, she is pleased that she does not have to pay a fixed amount each week but what she can when she can. The Family Service Unit adviser has helped her apply for a social fund grant for redecoration, but, for this reason, she will not accept a loan if offered: 'The room and the home will just have to stay as it is.'

Anjum does not have the money to keep up with repairs and maintenance on her house: the bathroom is still damp and the whole house needs redecorating. She would like to do up one of the bedrooms for her older son – who wants his own room – but cannot afford wallpaper, carpet and furniture for it.

Clothes are another problem; she goes without for herself, but the children are always needing them. At the moment, the whole family needs winter coats and the older boy needs shoes, but she is simply unable to afford them.

LANGUAGE DIFFICULTIES

Anjum cannot speak or write English well. She dislikes the dependence this causes – she has to find someone to help her fill in forms, or go to the DSS or to the solicitor who is dealing with her divorce. She also worries that she may receive important letters and not understand them:

> If you don't pay bills they take you to court. They'll send maybe one notice but won't wait to send more.

Partly because she is unable to make herself understood, she does not feel able to use buses and if she has to go outside the local area – for example to hospital – she has to take a taxi. She also has problems understanding the letters the children bring home from school, although as a result of English classes her understanding is increasing. But she finds it difficult to learn, partly because of other stresses.

CONTACTS WITH THE DSS

Anjum's benefit book has sometimes been delayed; even a week's delay is traumatic when money is this short. The DSS has taken her husband to court and she thinks he is paying maintenance direct to them.

Her main problem with the DSS is that they provide no interpreting or translation service, even though she lives in an area with a very large Asian community, many of whom, like her, speak Punjabi. Every time she has to fill in a form or needs to go to the DSS office, she has to ask for help. She has no idea how the DSS calculates what it gives her.

EXCLUSION

Anjum does see local friends, but otherwise she cannot afford to go out or visit relatives in another town. She gets lonely sitting at home and would like to get out of the house.

She particularly regrets that she is unable to afford to take the children on outings and, as a result, tries very hard to meet the charges for school trips:

> I'm not able to take them out anywhere, so these school trips, when other children go, they [children] say they should go too.

In addition, as the children grow up their demands become more expensive – eg, they want more fashionable clothes. This is another pressure.

STRESS

Anjum's children are healthy, although the youngest had an operation for a hole in the heart when a baby. She herself suffers from headaches and is losing weight. Anjum worries a great deal about how shortage of money affects the children. She is anxious about their future and about how she will keep up the repayments on the home, so 'it just goes round and round in my head'. She finds it especially painful when the children pester her for things she just cannot provide.

Anjum considers that, in spite of all these difficulties, she is better off without her husband: 'Yes, it [the money] isn't enough but . . . at least there is no nagging, no arguments, no pressure.' Nevertheless, in many ways she finds her situation depressing:

> I have to cope, with difficulty. But life is nothing, it hasn't been so far and I don't think it will be in the future.

However, the children's well-being is her absolute priority:

> I'm sitting here for the children and it's for the children first.

She hopes that later on, when her English is better and they are older, she will be able to get work to fit in with school hours.

STORY SIX:
'CARPETS AREN'T NECESSARY': GEOFFREY BOULD

Geoffrey Bould is 35 and recently separated. His council house is in poor condition – the windows are draughty and:

> in winter the house is freezing. I only have an electric heater. The plaster on the walls is crumbling.

Geoffrey suffers from hepatitis B and bronchitis. Although he feels better off financially than before his separation, he still has not got enough money and this creates strains and tensions:

> If I get down for a few days over money worries, it aggravates my bronchitis.

Work is the obvious solution to this problem, but he is not optimistic. Geoffrey has been unemployed for seven years – despite going on a Restart course – and all he's been offered is a Restart type of job at £36 per week and 'there's no way I'm going to take that'. He'd like a good enough wage to be able to keep his partner and daughter, and says they would then come back to him. To do this and pay his bills and rent, he considers that he would need about £150 per week. Also, for health reasons, he needs an outside job. In the meantime, because 'they' show no signs of helping him into work, he does irregular casual work.

MONEY AND BUDGETING

Money is a constant source of worry and Geoffrey has nothing to fall back on in terms of savings or insurance. Before his partner left they had recently become entitled to a weekly £2 rise in benefit but:

> it was no help, it just paid for the water. Every time they put it up, you have to fork out more for bills.

In recent years, the only time he has had any money was when his partner cashed in an insurance policy, which they spent on things for the house. He has no vacuum cleaner, freezer, telephone or car, and his iron and washing machine are in poor condition.

His partner left (with their child) the previous year, after sharing his present house for 18 months. He is still in close touch with them; indeed, she usually does his big shop for him and, if he has a little bit of money at the end of the week, he normally spends it on his daughter. They all spent Christmas together, with a food hamper which they had saved up for together at £40 per month for a few months. He had also managed to save enough to buy some 'little things' for his daughter. They had separated originally because of money problems; in fact, at present, both he and his girlfriend now feel better off claiming separately:

> Lack of money got us down – it put a strain on our relationship. We used to end up with about £60-odd per fortnight for the three of us.

When he is short of money for something, Geoffrey will miss paying a bill for that week or a couple of friends or relatives will lend him money. Although he dislikes having to go to them, he sometimes has to, and the amount he owes them is increasing all the time. Relatives also gave him and his partner some furniture and furnishings when they got their first council flat. They were refused a single payment then, both for furniture and clothes for the baby, who had just been born. His partner's social worker wrote to the DSS but they were still turned down. They were told that 'carpets weren't necessary'. As a result, they went to Catholic Housing Aid for furniture and to the WRVS for clothes for the child. Geoffrey felt grateful and angry at the same time:

> . . . [angry] with myself that I couldn't afford to buy them, just as I now feel pissed off at having to go to charity shops for the little girl because I can't afford to buy new clothes for her.

If he had an extra £5 per week, 'that's where it would go, on things for her'.

Despite feeling a little better off financially now, he still finds it very hard to meet bills, especially the water rates. He got into arrears and the court wrote to him. He said he could afford no more than £2 a week but they demanded £16 per month. He does not think he will be able to afford this amount.

When Geoffrey was with his girlfriend, the electricity used to be paid by direct deduction. Since she left, he has asked for fuel costs to be deducted from benefit, but this has yet to be organised and he has not been able to put anything aside for bills.

To meet the bills, something always has to give. When he and his girlfriend were together, the week the water rates were due, he had to make the child go without something such as an item of clothing or even shoes. Now:

> I'm not bothered about going out . . . Well, it's not worth letting it bother you.

He does not have holidays, wears mainly second-hand clothes, has only one pair of shoes and a pair of trainers, and no best outfit – and he does not go out. He needs a new bed, but simply does not have the money.

CONTACTS WITH THE DSS

Geoffrey feels that DSS officials have never offered him support. When his girlfriend left, he changed to claiming as a single man. The social security office took two and a half weeks to sort out his benefit and he was eventually forced to apply for a crisis loan from the social fund. 'I just took what was offered.' This was £14, repayable at over £5 per week:

> The level of repayments was ridiculous: I argued with them but it was to no avail. I had to take it because I had no money or food in the house. I just *had* to accept it. £10.50 was gone from my first giro and I had to borrow £10 from a friend which also had to be paid back that first week, so I had almost nothing left after I paid back what I owed.

He felt resentful both because he knew people getting bigger loans who were paying back the same sorts of repayments and because his girlfriend was treated much more generously:

> The officials weren't helpful. There were delays and hassles . . . they talk to you all right but they tell lies, they don't seem to be interested.

Similarly, when the couple split up, Geoffrey told the council he needed a new book for his general rates but, seven months later, he had heard nothing back. He assumes there will be a big bill when they do finally get round to contacting him. He has strong views regarding the social security system as a whole: 'they should blow the whole lot up and get a new lot in'.

TRAPPED AND RESENTFUL

Geoffrey appears trapped and dragged down by his environment and by the failure of the system to create the right opportunities; he is increasingly desperate and resentful and takes out his frustration on the only people within reach – local officials and his neighbours:

> This area is out of control with kids and dogs. All the best people have gone. There's no point in improving the houses, people will only make a mess of them.

And in line with his general experience of the 'system':

> the council are useless – they won't do repairs.

Despite his desire to better himself, Geoffrey feels frustrated by circumstances over which he has no control.

3 Budgeting on benefit

It is obvious that most of these families . . . cannot obtain the basic needs of spiritually and physically healthy lives . . . In a household in which deficiency plays a far larger part than fulfilment, it is certain that the mother, who is the chancellor of the family exchequer, will deprive herself, instinctively or deliberately, for the sake of her husband and children.

Working Class Wives, Margery Spring Rice, 1939

In this chapter we look at how claimants managed their money: how they coped with weekly budgeting and lump-sum expenses; what they had to do without; and how they viewed their standard of living. Given that the interviews took place in 1989/90, to some extent we are able to make an evaluation of how this part of the overhaul of the social security system affected income support claimants and how far the changes seemed to be achieving the aims set for them.

HARD TIMES GETTING HARDER

In general, it was common for claimants who had been on benefit long-term to say they found it more and more difficult to manage. Sandra (see Chapter 2) explained that when she was working she used to buy the children's clothes at Marks and Spencer, but soon after she started living on benefit she found she could not afford it:

When Woolworth's started to improve their standards I started buying there, but even Woolworth's have got expensive now so I'm literally down to going to the market . . . something I would never have done. I just buy in the market, things fall apart in no time.

We interviewed the claimants twice in the FSU study – in 1989 and 1990. Two-thirds of those still on benefit (24 out of 36) reported that they considered themselves worse off in 1990 than in the previous year. The most common explanation for this situation was that the benefit increase had not kept pace with inflation. However, a number of people also found that their expenses were increasing as children got older. (Income support rates for children do not increase until the children reach the age of 11.) Several parents who had new babies during the year had also found it difficult to meet the resulting extra expenses.

For example, Jim and Marie Denton, with four children to clothe and feed, said it was 'a bit harder' to manage in 1990 than in 1989. Mrs Denton reported:

> The money has gone up but it's still not gone up anywhere near the cost of living . . . I've not actually got any money left over to go out and buy, like, say, shoes . . . [Q. And did you, last year?] . . . Well, you were maybe able to keep enough back – a couple of extra pounds or something – then in two weeks, three weeks we had a pair of shoes.

Lucille Jeffreys, a single mother, commented:

> When my money went up from the £59 to the £63 I thought, oh, I've got a bit more money now, but it didn't go any further.

Lucille took on a social fund loan for things she needed because she moved and, as a result, had £3.25 deducted from her benefit each week:

> It's so difficult – even though it's just like £3 odd – but I'm finding that at the end of the week I'm stuck. You know what I mean? I've been borrowing off my mother and everything . . . Definitely more, I don't know why, I'm just spending more. I think it's also because the kids are getting bigger as well. They need more food, they're eating more. . . .

BUDGETING WEEK TO WEEK

Faced with reduced purchasing power, claimants had to make some hard choices about what to spend money on. In the context of an inadequate income, even the most careful budgeting only results in the satisfaction of one need at the expense of another. Thus a majority of the claimants interviewed confirmed that the exercise of their budgeting discretion often extended no further than deciding 'what to do without this week'.

CUTTING DOWN

Eighty-five out of the ninety-one people interviewed in Bradford stated that they regularly cut down on food and/or fuel. In the FSU study, claimants described similar budgeting strategies.

Cutting down on food usually involved reducing or foregoing such things as sweets, cakes, biscuits and fresh fruit and meat. Parents were particularly concerned that they could not provide what they saw as a healthy diet (see also Chapter 6). Nearly everyone interviewed felt that providing fresh meat was a priority; but even so it was common for claimants to say that they could rarely afford meat, or could only afford cheap cuts which were not nutritious. A young father explained:

> [in the supermarket] we have to go past the meat and pies and chicken, we have to leave them all behind.

Marie Denton commented:

> We can't afford fresh meat every day, be lucky if we get fresh meat once a week.

A number of pensioners and families with children also said that they were unable to use the heating as much as they wanted, often only heating one room in the house even in the coldest winter months. Over half the people in the FSU study said they economised on fuel. This included several whose flats were centrally-heated, but who never made use of this heating system because they were worried about the cost. Others never heated the bedrooms, or only turned on the heating when their children came home from school (Chapter 6 describes how this is linked to health problems).

Most people bought second-hand clothes for themselves, and sometimes also for their children, although parents would often try to ensure that the children, as far as possible, got new clothes, either going to jumble sales for themselves or just doing without. Many found this humiliating.

With few exceptions, people stated that they had no 'social' spending money for themselves and therefore never went out (see Chapter 5).

THE ELDERLY

The elderly, although defined as 'more' needy by policy-makers, were often unable to satisfy all their basic needs for food and fuel. Many used 'doing without' as one of their main strategies. Mrs Austin was typical of many when she explained that if she were to be given an extra £5 per week she would 'eat more food and have more heating and go out'.

As we have seen in Chapter 2, Mrs Austin could not afford the overnight heating, which she required for health reasons.

Mrs Wilson, an 80 year-old widow, received £45 per week after 'fuel direct' deductions from benefit for gas and electricity. She received no annual uprating in 1988 or 1989. She puts money aside for rates and water rates each week: 'the £10.60 a month (for water rates) has affected me badly.' Her daughter goes bulk shopping for her every week and, in spite of careful budgeting, Mrs Wilson still has no money left at the end of the week. She has no telephone or washing machine, not even an electric kettle. She needs carpets but cannot afford to repay a social fund loan.

Aside from her regular bills, Mrs Wilson also pays £1.50 per week to her 'clubman' for some kitchen lino. She has no other debts, and does not drink or go out in the evenings. She is practically housebound because of age and infirmity, suffering from an ulcer, chronic bronchitis and anaemia. Despite these problems she cannot use the gas fire as much as she wants: 'I feel cold often but you can't turn the gas fire on, it's too expensive.' She felt worse-off this year: 'Last year it wasn't too bad but this year everything has gone up – food prices have got too high, we have to watch everything we spend. I worry if the gas and electric bills go up. If I start worrying it affects my health. I keep thinking how I'm going to manage, that affects me.'

WHEN THE MONEY RUNS OUT

Despite careful planning, over two-thirds of the claimants in the Bradford and FSU studies stated that they were unable to afford to buy everything they needed each week and so regularly ran out of money before the next fortnight's benefit payment was due. Often the money for essentials, such as food, would just not stretch from one week's end to another. For example, a mother of four complained, 'I never have any money left in my purse . . . even though I don't smoke or drink.'

It was common to be forced into debt simply for regular weekly expenses like food and fuel. This applied to most claimants, although strategies for dealing with it often differed according to cultural background. White and Afro-Caribbean families would often borrow small amounts of money from friends and relatives outside the household. Asian claimants might get this kind of support, sometimes from a working relative living in the same house. More frequently, they bought things on credit from local Asian shops.

Amounts borrowed at the end of the week were nearly always paid back as soon as the next benefit payment arrived. This could be important as sometimes the friends or relations who lent money were themselves living on benefit, but perhaps paid on a different day. But this left the claimant 'short' again for the next week, resulting in further cut-backs. As one lone mother put it: 'The day after I'm paid I'm back to square one . . . '

GOING WITHOUT

When all else failed, people just had to go without – to 'tighten the stomach' as one woman put it. This often happened at the weekend (as Monday and Tuesday were common benefit paydays) and was particularly hard for those paid benefit fortnightly (where the claimant was signing on as unemployed). When the money ran out the family could be trapped in the home, with no money for any social activities (see Chapter 5). It was common for people to say that when this happened, 'we just sit quietly at home.'

Asian families said they would fall back on the staples of dhal and roti (lentils and bread) which they usually bought in bulk. Many people also cut down on food and other essentials like fuel. A couple with a two-year-old found that about every four or six weeks they were in danger of running out of money well before their fortnightly giro was due. When this happened:

> We'll have something like rice, cooked rice mixed with something else, really cheap food and we'll take £5 off the food money and buy something that way, or do without electricity for a couple of days . . . instead of going straight to the LEB [electricity board] we just leave it off and buy less [electricity] tokens . . . (we) put candles on, get candles out.

Anjum explained how she and her children managed:

> Sometimes I just say be quiet and sit indoors. If there is any dhal we will eat that and there is usually always flour so we will have dhal and roti.

THE EFFECTS ON MOTHERS

In both studies, a number of mothers said that they regularly missed meals or went short to make sure their children had enough food (see Chapter 2). It was common for women to say that when money was short they would live on toast and tea, or sandwiches, or finish up the children's leftovers. For example:

> I only eat once a day, usually at tea-time, if I feel like it. But I've got to the stage I say to myself I'm not hungry, I can go for days without nothing. [Q. Is that to save money?] It's because I want to put a bit decent in my bairns' stomach.

> I try to put things together, you know, what's left in the cupboards, or sometimes I go to bed with a cup of tea or some bread . . . If I just have enough to give the kids I'll just have a cup of tea and that's it . . . When I feed them, when I've got the food to give them they always say oh, my tummy is very full and I feel so good about that, but sometimes I just have tea.

> We only have meat three times a week – one night I have to give him beans on toast. I feel awful about this . . . I don't cook for myself . . . if he leaves any I eat that . . . today I had toast.

> I make sure the children eat first; if there's any left, I will. If not . . . then it doesn't matter about me.

In some cases, the effects of general stress were combined with lack of money – women who regularly went short or without did not feel like eating anyway (see Chapter 5). For example, Marie Denton – who said she survived for 'days on end' on tea and coffee – went on to explain that she was not able to buy the food she liked:

> I buy it for them, because it's like I'm a minority in this house, a lot of them eat a lot of things which I do without to feed the rest of them.

Jim described her as 'a picky eater' but she explained how she handled balancing her needs and those of the four children:

> I'm a cheese fan. I'd eat cheese every day of the week, except that cheese is expensive . . . I usually buy a pound of cheese on a Thursday or half a pound on a Thursday and half a pound on a Friday and that just lasts me the day and that's it, that's my quota.

BUDGETING FOR LARGE EXPENSES

We found that, in practice, the withdrawal of single payment grants seemed to have done little to encourage independence and good budgeting practices. Weekly benefit levels were not high enough to allow claimants to budget effectively even for regular weekly expenses, let alone to cover expensive household items such as carpets, cookers and the like or to replace children's clothing. As a result, the abolition of single payments seems to have had serious consequences for the people interviewed. In the first place, for those who had taken out loans, there was the increased pressure on weekly income generated by social fund repayments. For many claimants, whether or not they had taken out loans, there was also a high level of dependency on other agencies and institutions (usually, but not solely, the family) and high levels of unmet need for household items considered essential by the population at large. None of this had had the effect of encouraging greater 'self-reliance' or budgeting skill on the part of the claimant.

Claimants emphasised the impossibility of saving for lump sums out of weekly benefit. In Bradford, only three out of ninety-one claimants had any sort of savings. One of these was the remains of a redundancy payment, another was savings for the couple's own funerals and the last was a very small amount remaining after a lifetime's saving while in work. In the FSU study, too, savings were virtually non-existent. Some people did save in the very short-term – putting away a little for a few weeks for children's shoes, or to pay fuel bills – but they often also spoke of having to break into money saved in this way when an unexpected expense became urgent.

USE OF THE SOCIAL FUND

Only a third (35 out of 91) of the Bradford interviewees had made one or more applications to the social fund during its first 24 months. Of these, six were Asian. The majority of these applications were for budgeting loans. Out of a total of 57 social fund applications, half (28) were refused or resulted in awards which the applicant found unacceptable and rejected. Of 36 budgeting loan applications, only eight resulted in a full payment and a further 13 in a part-payment. The remainder were refused by the DSS (12), rejected by the claimant (two) or were pending (one). Of the ten applications for community care grants (CCGs) only two were actually awarded. A small number of applications were for crisis loans, usually following relationship breakdown, change of claim (with resultant delay in receiving normal benefit) or theft/fire.

The picture from the FSU study was slightly different, in part because the interviewees had had regular access to help and advice from social workers and others at their local Family Service Units. A similar proportion to that in Bradford (13 out of 45) had received budgeting loans by the first interview in autumn 1989, but in addition three had received CCGs by then and seven more grants were awarded by 1990. All but two of these were for expenses associated with a move, and advice from a social worker or other professional played a crucial part in obtaining the grant. In both the FSU and the Bradford studies, it was very unusual for an Asian family to take on a social fund loan and many did not know about them. For example, of the 57 households in Bradford *not* applying to the social fund, ten (nine of them Asian) were unaware of the option. It was common not to want to take on the extra commitment which would lead to less weekly money. For example, Anjum Abbas had been persuaded by the community worker to apply for a CCG. She had decided she would not accept a loan if that was what was offered:

It's not worth it if they take it out of the benefit . . . with another loan it's too much.

Rashid Chaudry had a similar reaction:

[It's an] extra burden. I couldn't afford to take on something else like that. I have enough worries already.

While a social fund loan solved the immediate problem of purchasing something the claimant needed, the burden of paying back the loan simply shifted the basic problem of insufficient money to another sphere. In the FSU study, it was clear that taking up social fund loans was associated with getting into debt. In 1989, twenty-two out of forty-five claimants had multiple debts (ie three or more), and this included all but one of the thirteen who were repaying social fund loans. While it is impossible to separate completely the effect of social fund loan repayment from the general effects of living on an inadequate income, a significant number of Bradford households also ascribed their worsening situation to social fund loan repayments.

For those on benefit income, even a relatively small deduction plays havoc with finances. Lucille Jeffreys, who had taken out a loan for expenses linked to a move (see above) found even £3.25 per week crippling:

It was only last month that I took it [SF deduction] off. I would say the beginning of last month, even though it doesn't seem like that long, it seems like a century . . . I've really noticed it, it's really hit me.

DEBT AND BUDGETING STRATEGIES

In Bradford, around half the white British claimants already made regular repayments out of their weekly benefit – for example, to clubmen, catalogues for children's clothes and small household items. Often they could barely afford the repayments on these and therefore had to miss regular bill payments to make ends meet.

Their situation had been particularly acute since the introduction of the new requirements to pay 20 per cent of rates and water rates. Twenty of the Bradford claimants had rates arrears, including 11 families with children; in the FSU study this was the commonest type of debt (17 out of 45 claimants). Altogether, half the Bradford claimants already made regular repayments out of their weekly benefit, on top of their standard bills. Two out of three of the FSU claimants had debts of some kind.

Almost all Asian families in the Bradford interviews had debts to local shops for clothes and furniture bought on tick. While very few were in arrears with bills and rates, they only managed to keep up with these payments by getting into more debt with local shops in the weeks that bills were paid. Asian families in the FSU study also tended to take out private loans – generally quite reluctantly, but often for fairly large amounts – from friends or relatives. But there was an absolute obligation to repay these commitments. Anjum's response to a £500 loan she felt forced to take for household repairs (see Chapter 2) was typical:

> My big worry is that the people I borrowed [from] might come knocking on my door for it. Though they're good people, still they themselves might need it for a hundred things, then what will I do? Honestly, sometimes I can't sleep at night for thinking about it. A loan of one penny from anybody is worrying, but this is £500.

For those whose existing debts left no scope for further economies in the weekly budget, social fund repayments could only be financed by taking on further debt. For example, one couple with three children already paid a substantial amount of their weekly benefit in catalogue repayments – for children's clothes, shoes and small household items. With a great deal of careful budgeting they managed to keep up with these commitments. However, when they moved house they needed to buy new beds and a cooker and so applied for a social fund loan. The resulting repayments upset the fine balance of their weekly budget: they simply could not afford them. The result was that they had to take out a finance company loan to keep up, with the money now used to repay the social fund loan. As a result of the delayed repayment scheme and 45 per cent interest rates on the finance company loan, they were still repaying this debt long after the social fund loan had been repaid. This resulted in considerable hardship to the family. The slide into debt does little to increase claimants' self-reliance.

> I wish we'd never applied for the loan . . . it left us more in debt . . . Our relatives have to offer to help us with our telephone bill and the commission he gets at Christmas from a hamper club will have to be used to pay off the catalogue debts.

MIKE GOLDWATER/NETWORK

'I dream about finding the back door of Marks & Spencers open and going in and just picking up all the things I want . . . this will do for Jenny, and that for Darren . . . I'd like to be able to give them what other children have without having to juggle and make them plod on, but there's no choice.'

A number of mothers stated that the money being used to repay social fund loans would have been used to buy things for their children. A lone parent with four children who received a social fund loan for a bed and a cooker said, 'I could have used this money for shoes for the kids, they always need shoes.' Another mother of four paying off loans for a cooker, gas fire and washing machine reported 'we're £7.50 down on weekly money.'

WHAT KIND OF DEPENDENCE?

As we have seen, one government aim in reforming social security was to reduce dependence on state provision. In practice, though, this dependence seems to have been transferred elsewhere – for example, to the family. Whether or not they had used the social fund, many of the claimants we saw were dependent on relatives. As well as supplying the needs of claimants who had been refused by, or put off applying to, the social fund, families also often 'picked up the pieces' of a weekly budget depleted by social fund loan repayments.

HELP FROM FAMILIES

Almost half the non-Asian families with dependent children in Bradford stated that relatives frequently gave the children gifts of clothes or shoes. Similar findings emerged from the FSU study.

Mr Downing described a typical situation:

> When we couldn't afford to buy shoes for the kids [the] wife's sister bought them . . . She said just call it their Christmas present . . . it was essential, no way could we have afforded it.

As noted before, Asian claimants were reluctant to make use of either social fund loans or loan companies. In general, those who sought help turned to family or friends for loans, particularly for important events like a daughter's wedding. However, as a claimant put it 'not all relatives are sympathetic or suitable for advice on financial matters' and, in any case, often 'there is no point – everyone seems in the same boat.' Several expressed considerable concern about the possibility of having to borrow: one widow 'prayed to God it won't happen'. In any case, in communities where many households were unemployed (as was typically the case within both communities studied) this might simply result in placing the burden of debt on other similarly-placed families.

Families also compensated for the loss of single payment grants more directly, by supplying essential items like furniture and carpets to claimants who had either been refused a loan, or had not applied for one. Over half of the non-Asian claimants interviewed in Bradford had received help from families in this way.

With Asian households it tended to be more common for parents either to supply furniture and household goods when a son or daughter got married and set up home or, occasionally, if the young couple lived with parents, to share furniture and household goods. Under other circumstances, this kind of help was often not available.[1]

HOW IT FELT

Those forced into borrowing from or depending on family help felt themselves pulled in two directions. While claimants were grateful for this type of assistance, the implied dependency often put a strain on wider family relationships and decreased self-esteem. Maria, a 41-year-old lone parent with one teenager, expressed frustration over her dependent position. She works part-time and her wages are set against her income support, allowing her to keep only £15 per week. Even so, she only just manages to keep her head above water, because she is paying off old debts accumulated when she was forced to move after a relationship breakdown. Maria needs all manner of household essentials, such as a carpet, lino, a vacuum cleaner and decorating materials – 'it's soul-destroying, the state of the house' – but she cannot afford to get further into debt for these items. While feeling grateful to her sister who gave her her old carpets she also 'resents' this situation and the inequality it implies. 'She [sister] could just afford to toss it away, go out and buy a new one and think nothing of it.' Maria feels as though her relatives resent the gifts and so the strain is two-way.

Jane Wright, with an unemployed husband and four children, said they would ask her mother for help but, typically, added that they would have to be desperate to do so:

If it was something for the kid, I mean if I was desperate for shoes for say, the youngest, I could say to my ma; she'd say 'Right, bring her up' and she'd go and get her the shoes.

[Q. Would you feel okay about that?]

As long as she took [back] the money it'd be okay but my ma tends to say sometimes it doesn't matter and I feel guilty, with her being a pensioner, I feel I'm taking it out of my ma's pocket, you know what I mean, she needs it herself. But I'd need to be really desperate before I'd go.

As we have seen, Asian parents on income support often found it impossible to save enough for a child's wedding and the gifts of household goods which tradition demands. This resulted in them taking loans for large amounts of money from other relatives – itself often a source of humiliation – and then feeling the shame of not being able to repay.

A few claimants in the FSU study had access via social workers to help from charities. This could also feel degrading. For example, Jim and Marie Denton needed a new washing machine. Two of their children were incontinent and Marie was allergic to soap powder which made hand-washing a real problem. There was no launderette within reach. After managing soiled bed-linen for months without a machine, they were persuaded to accept help from a charity. Marie hated this situation, but they both helped out at the FSU as a way of 'paying back.' Other claimants spoke about having to turn to FSU for help when money ran out – for example, when the giro did not arrive:

That's not really the place to lend me money like that, they're for emergencies . . . (it's) like begging from them, whereas the social or somebody should be giving you it.

UNMET NEED

Fifty-six of the 91 households in Bradford had made no application to the social fund and 26 of these were Asian households (from the total of 32 Asian households interviewed). However, it was clear that lack of 'take-up' did not equate with an absence of need. Only four families gave 'needing nothing' as their reason for not applying to the social fund; apart from those who did not know about the fund, virtually all of the remaining 42 families did not want to apply for a loan for a variety of reasons. Similarly, in the FSU study two-thirds of the claimants had not applied, but in many cases this was also a conscious decision.

Lack of knowledge about the social fund was a factor particularly for Asian claimants. In both studies, a substantial proportion of Asian households did not know about the fund. However, those who did were sceptical about repayable loans for much the same reasons as other claimants. By far the most common reason for not applying to the social fund was the perceived impossibility of paying back a loan out of weekly benefit. This was generally based on a sound assessment of the level of repayments possible, given a very limited weekly budget. Having already made cut-backs in weekly consumption to meet other debts, claimants often saw no other choice but to do without the needed item. One pensioner remarked 'they'd take it back out of my weekly money and I couldn't afford to pay for anything else, I wouldn't be able to eat.'

Some pensioners were reluctant to apply to the social fund because they found the process of making a special application for some essential items degrading. Given, in most cases, a life-time of national insurance contributions, they failed to see why they should have to make a special application for some basic item they needed. One pensioner expressed a common view:

> I prefer to do without, I don't like begging.

Like other pensioners, Mrs Austin did not want to apply to the DSS:

> I might as well save up myself . . . If I can't afford a thing I'll do with-
> out . . . I'd get hire purchase rather than bother with social security.

Other people felt that it was pointless making an application. From what they had heard of local office priorities, they were unlikely to be successful in obtaining anything except possibly a crisis loan.

Interestingly, very few claimants seemed to consider the possibility of a community care grant (CCG). This was either because they were unaware of this possibility or because they did not believe they would be entitled. Of those in the FSU study who did apply for grants, most, as we have seen, were helped by social workers or other professionals. In the Bradford study only two households had been offered and accepted a grant. One family was originally offered a loan, converted to a grant after an intervention by the mother's social worker. The other was a lone parent moving from a homeless person's hostel in another town to set up home for the first time, with no furniture or furnishings.

A quarter of all those in the FSU households moved in the year covered by the interviews and many of their lump-sum needs were associated with such moves. Other people were either setting up home for the first time or trying to refurnish a home after some major event – for example, relationship breakdown, fire, theft, or illness – had depleted their resources. Still others simply needed to replace worn-out furniture, cookers or other household items. Some were pensioners who, after a lifetime of work both in and out of the home, had been left frail and isolated without any form of family support.

Second-hand furniture stores were used extensively and items were bought second-hand from friends. While other families tended to buy more second-hand clothes, Asians tended to buy new (but the cheapest) clothes, usually on tick. Since 1980, the availability of lump-sum payments for clothing has steadily been curtailed[2] but clothing, particularly for children, remained a major lump-sum need for these claimants. Even after all avenues had been explored, claimants reported that they did not have some of the basic items that the wider population takes for granted. While fear of debt had the effect of 'filtering out' many potential social fund applications, thereby reducing the burden on the state, the effect on the claimants was one of increasing deprivation rather than increasing independence.

DEPRIVATION

Claimants reported worryingly high levels of unmet need. In the FSU study, families were doing without many of the common household goods for which single payment grants had formerly been made. People were living with dangerous cookers which they could not afford to replace or repair; children were sharing beds; wardrobes and chests of drawers were often lacking. Redecoration was also often needed, not as a matter of taste but of necessity, but could not be afforded.

The Bradford study looked in detail at the household goods and other items which families possessed. At the time of interview, claimants were missing not only essential items such as furniture and bedding (half of all claimants stated that they needed one or more of this type of item) but also many essential household durables.

On average, families with children had access to only eight of the items on the 12-item list, missing essentials such as irons, vacuum cleaners, fridges and cookers. The picture for pensioners was similar: on average, they had access to only seven of the standard items. Childless families reported the least access to these items, on average having only six of the items (see Appendix for list).

Levels of ownership of consumer durables reflected not only the general poverty of those interviewed but also different patterns of ownership resulting from culturally-shaped preferences. Thus, telephone (42 per cent), freezer (26 per cent) and car (13 per cent) ownership was considerably lower than levels in the population at large. On the other hand, while 75 per cent of non-Asian families owned an electric kettle, only 9 per cent of the Asian families did so (as they are less essential for culinary purposes). Conversely, ownership of videos and cars was significantly higher in the Asian group of interviewees than in the white British. The former reflects the desire of the Pakistani respondents to be able to see own-language films, and to compensate for the lack of easily available films appropriate for Muslim viewers on mainstream TV programmes.

From a list of 12 items, Bradford families were also asked to state goods or services (see Appendix) which they had or did not have and, if the latter, whether this was because they were unable to afford them. Similar patterns were observed in the FSU study. Thus 75 per cent of all claimants said that they did not have regular (yearly) holidays because they could not afford them. Thirty-eight of the 59 non-Asian families could not afford even one night out a fortnight. However, only one-third of all non-Asian families could afford mostly new clothes whereas the corresponding proportion of Asian families was over four-fifths. Similarly, three-quarters of Asian households had two satisfactory hot meals each day; for other families, the proportion was again less than one-third.

Although the pattern of particular consumer goods owned varied from family to family, and between ethnic groups, overall there was very little difference between two-parent families and lone-parent families, or between Asian families and others. As a group, lone parents had marginally lower levels of overall ownership of durables but marginally higher access to items, goods and services than two-parent families with children. In general, these patterns suggest different priorities for weekly (and annual) budgeting within the same fixed incomes for different ethnic groups, although the underlying difficulty – of juggling priorities and doing without various essential items – was common to the two groups.

CHOICES IN BUDGETING

Rashid Chaudry spoke for many others when he responded to a question about what the family needed but were unable to afford:

> We just do without and live like this.

For those who did apply to the social fund, it seemed to offer little assistance. Making loan repayments out of depleted benefit meant that the social fund became part of the problem of increasing debt and hardship. In this context, the concept of budgeting skill, which implies the scope to make choices, became meaningless.

For those who did not apply to the social fund, the same problem remained; benefit levels were too low to allow them to meet their needs in any other way. Increased dependency, debt or deprivation were the only choices to be made.

REFERENCES

1   Sadiq-Sangster, A, (1991), *Living on income support: an Asian experience*, Family Service Units, London.
2   Cohen, R, and Tarpey, M, (eds), (1988), *Single payments: the disappearing safety net*, Poverty Pamphlet No 74, CPAG Ltd, London.

4 Staking your claim

You feel poor because you're poor, you don't feel part of the system . . . You feel like you're shoved in the corner, you're just an extra statistic . . . because I'm not contributing nothing. You feel like you're having to beg from the system to get something out of the government to survive . . . If the system was different, where you could work and we could afford to work, contribute to our children, live happy, pay our way, I think everyone would have a different attitude . . . The worst thing about being on social security is that it takes away your pride, people treat you different . . . they don't treat you as a person.

Melanie Baker

This chapter examines how the families interviewed experienced the social security system itself. We look at their perceptions of the way it is administered; how claimants felt about the way in which they were treated and how that affected their self-image; and their comments about the experience of being on the receiving end of the management and delivery of benefits. First, though, we explain how the DSS organisation itself has changed.

ORGANISATIONAL CHANGE

In recent years, there has been considerable criticism of the quality and effectiveness of social security administration as well as of its cost.[1] Supplementary benefit (until 1988) and income support have consistently been far more expensive to administer than any other social security benefit, except the social fund.

Administrative change has increasingly been overshadowed by the phased introduction of a computerised system for the administration and delivery of social security benefits. With installation costs to be balanced in part by savings in staffing levels, it was originally estimated that at least 20,000 jobs within local offices were to be cut. As a result, throughout the 1980s, there was a growing emphasis on postal claiming, and self-assessment within application forms. This was a *de facto* recognition that growing pressure on staff – particularly at a time of rapidly increasing unemployment and a relative decline in staffing levels – meant, for example, that home visiting by social security staff was bound to have a low priority. Throughout the 1980s and into the 1990s, about 250,000 home visits per year had to be abandoned by social security staff due to pressure of work. This trend increasingly placed the onus on claimants to understand the benefit system and pursue their rights themselves – something which was often difficult enough for those familiar with the social security system and the English language, but considerably more difficult for those for whom Britain was not a first home nor English a first language.[2]

In the past few years, a number of steps have also been taken in response to criticisms of institutional and individual racism within the social security system. One of the local offices to have benefited most from these changes was the Westfield House office which served the area in which many of Bradford's Asian claimants live. By 1990, this office offered a number of services including full-time interpretation (in Urdu and Punjabi) and liaison. However, the interpreter only wrote in English and translation into other written languages had to be carried out at another office. Very few DSS offices elsewhere have even comparable facilities. Nationally, major leaflets had been made available in seven languages apart from English and an 'ethnic freeline' telephone service was being piloted as our studies came to a conclusion.

For Asian claimants with language difficulties, a lack of understanding and awareness of the changes to the social security system was even more pronounced than that of claimants in general. For example, almost none of the Bradford Asian claimants knew about premiums, compared with over half of the other claimants. Most of these claimants were receiving the premiums to which they were entitled – especially those with simpler qualifying rules, such as pensioner or lone-parent premiums. But several families were not getting the more unusual premiums to which they would have been entitled, such as the various disability premiums (see also Chapter 6).

It was also true that a significant proportion of claimants, especially Asians, were unaware of the social fund. Where they knew about particular benefits or the fund, it seemed as likely that they had heard through word of mouth as that they had been told by officials that they might qualify. Indeed, several claimants had to engage in lengthy arguments to establish their eligibility against the protestations of social security officials.

One lone parent had heard of the social fund on a TV programme, but had no real idea of what it involved:

> It's a horrible name apart from anything else I think . . . it sounds very like charity. And income support I think is not nearly as nice a term as . . . I mean neither of them are nice terms but I think supplementary benefit is a better term than income support . . . because of the words, the connotations of the word support, yes, the government is supporting you . . .

Claimants in both studies were asked about their experience of the claiming process and of the social security system. For example, claimants in Bradford were asked both whether the changes had made it easier to understand which benefits they were entitled to and, at the end of the interview, whether they had any general comments to make about the social security system as a whole. Most claimants expressed forthright views (by no means all negative) about benefit administration, derived from their own experience or that of friends, neighbours and relatives. However, the overwhelming impression was of a generally profound lack of understanding. Even given the fact that a new system takes a while to 'bed down', the depth of misunderstanding or confusion (and the hostility and lack of trust which this causes or exacerbates) must be a cause for concern to a department preoccupied with customer satisfaction.

One disabled woman pensioner's comment was typical:

> No, I don't know what I'm entitled to really. You don't know where you are really with it (the new system) . . . I don't understand why they reduced my pension, they didn't give me any explanation.

Nor, indeed, was it clear to the interviewer whether the loss of the interviewee's weekly benefit income was due to loss of additional requirements (extra weekly payments), the shift to the premium system, the belief that pensioners were less favoured by the redistribution of social security resources in 1988, or some other factor.

BARRIERS TO UNDERSTANDING

A number of claimants, particularly those for whom the use of official English presented difficulties, had turned to others for help in interpreting (either language or the workings of the system); these others included local MPs, friends, relatives and local advice workers. An Asian couple with three children was amongst this group:

> No, it's not easier . . . I had to go to the advice centre to find out what I was entitled to and for the boy . . . It's not really clear how they work it out for each person because everybody gets different . . .

In this case, reference to the experiences of the husband's friends had offered no ground rules for assessment of his own benefit entitlement.

For such claimants, lack of appropriate translation or interpreting facilities at most local offices was a further obstacle both to understanding and claiming. Anjum, a lone parent, commented:

> Even if I was entitled to anything else, I don't know about it and then there is the problem of claiming. I don't like to ask people to do this [translate] for me.

Using hard-pressed local advice centres, however helpful, was not necessarily seen as an adequate substitute for an improved and appropriate service at the local social security office. Khalid, a father of several children, suggested:

> I don't know how to apply and it takes such a long time to go to the advice centre and get the form filled in and it's too much problems. I don't understand why my brother, who has the same number of children, gets more help than me . . .

And Anjum, otherwise an independent mother, admitted:

> The biggest problem is the language. I can understand it but when it comes to speaking it, I have to take someone with me. First I have to find the person or go to the FSU and ask them to either go with me or fill out the form.

The emphasis on postal claiming and self-assessment also led to difficulties for claimants who did not speak good English, particularly if there were literacy problems. In very many cases, the demand for assistance was felt by local advice workers who had to take on what many thought was properly the responsibility of the DSS.

For other claimants, whose grasp of English was adequate, the lack of contact with social security was deliberate and derived from their earlier and painful experiences. One blind 79-year-old had applied for an additional requirement (extra weekly payment) several years earlier. The DSS visitor told him to wash his clothes in the sink. 'I showed him the door and I've had nothing to do with them since.' Similarly, a man with disabilities had not recovered from his feelings about the way he was treated by the DSS when he lost his son in a cot death. He had asked social security to take over his electricity payments, but kept getting final demands from Yorkshire Electricity and social security would not reply to his letters asking for clarification. On the day his son was being buried, he received a letter telling him his benefit was being reduced.

A number of claimants' suspicions that they were being underpaid were also influenced by earlier experiences. As we have noted, many claimants lost heating, diet and laundry additions in 1988 but were not clear why or how (or indeed whether) that loss had been adjusted for in the new system – particularly as the notion of premiums was unfamiliar to the majority. In fact some were clearly not receiving premiums and had apparently been adjudged not severely disabled enough, for example, to be entitled to the financial compensation that award of a premium would bring. Even where disability premiums *were* being paid, families found it difficult to make the connection between the old and new ways of paying for certain needs. One older couple and their adult son, who was disabled as a result of meningitis, were in receipt of invalid care allowance and attendance allowance. However, they had lost weekly heating and laundry allowances for their son in 1988. In their case, they were not only confused but also fearful, as a result of local 'popular' perceptions of claimants:

> We can't understand anything. People are frightened to claim for things in case you're done for false claiming.

A fear which, in their case, was clearly inappropriate. They and other families did not even enquire about other entitlements and forewent possible increases in benefit rather than be labelled as scroungers or even fraudulent claimers.

CONTACT WITH OFFICIALS

For some, the lack of understanding of the benefits system was one result of the move away from personal contact and home visiting. The increasing stress on postal and computerised claiming had been noted by a few households, especially those claiming for some time. They regretted the loss of personal contact:

> They're not bad . . . but they don't visit families like they used to . . . That wasn't bad, at least you feel they're taking an interest in whether you're going out to work or if you're still managing on social security. It was a lot better.

One couple also reflected on the importance of home visiting in 'fine-tuning' assessments, something which was increasingly becoming the responsibility of the claimant and, as we have noted, was likely to lead to under-claiming. The wife reflected:

> I preferred it with the old system when the lad or lassie used to come out if you were needing a grant . . . It's not so formal, they came to your house to visit you, you say what you needed the money for, they decided whether you needed a bit extra for what you were asking for, or a bit lower . . . I preferred that because it's none of this letters here and forms there, you were on a one-to-one basis. So if they thought you're not really needing it, they said it to your face and not through a daft letter . . .

In fact, most direct contact with officials now seemed to be as a result of changing circumstances (with many claimants needing help from the DSS to cope with situations such as moves or crises – eg, relationship breakdowns), or of chasing up errors or delays. This often led to hostile exchanges because of tension and worry, which, as we describe below, often took place in a depressing or intimidating environment.

Some families had virtually given up trying to get to grips with the system in the face of past failures to gain what they saw as their rights. One couple with a husband who had disabilities had applied for attendance allowance and mobility allowance at different times

MIKE ABRAHAMS/NETWORK

'I think the real problem about being on the dole is that it destroys your self-esteem. I would really like to have a job where I could go out and earn some money and have a sense of achievement at the end of the day.'

in the past but failed to get either. Their sole success was to get a disabled person's bus pass (from the local authority). They had, however, lost weekly diet and heating allowances given prior to 1988:

> I don't know what we're entitled to . . . It's not a simple system. We don't know what we qualify for, we just hope for the best.

One lone parent had had a long-running battle with the DSS which had coloured her attitudes to claiming. She had been owed a lot of money by the DSS in 'fuel direct' payments and child benefit arrears; in each case, she had recovered these sums only after the intervention of the local Citizens' Advice Bureau. In her view, the DSS system was neither fair nor easily understandable:

> I don't know how they assess you but I know they don't assess you properly because a lot of people are getting ripped off by the system.

Lack of understanding of the benefits system was not infrequently turned into attacks on other claimants – in some cases directed at particular 'high-profile' groups of claimants such as black or Asian claimants or young unemployed people. For some, the social security system simply echoed wider divisions in society. One unemployed father commented on social security provision generally that 'the rich get richer and the poor get poorer.' For many more, however, the impression remained less of a rational and intelligible system than one which depended largely on chance and personal circumstances. As one older man with disabilities put it:

> When they changed to income support, I didn't get any information explaining the changes. I didn't really understand the changes, why I lost heating additions, they didn't explain it properly . . . It's no easier to understand. If anything it's harder . . . If you're lucky you get it, if you aren't you don't.

The social fund in particular was rightly regarded as a system in which chance played a major part in determining 'success'. In general, claimants did not understand the reasons for social fund decisions. Rules were seen as inflexible, and claimants believed that payments for certain items would always be refused or that they were bound not to receive the full amount for which they asked. On the other hand, variations in decisions were not perceived as indicating a flexible consideration of individual needs; instead they seemed to be impersonal and arbitrary.

WHAT DOES IT FEEL LIKE TO BE A CLAIMANT?

In the mind of the public, means-tested benefits have continued to be associated with feelings of stigma. This has been one of the major factors consistently leading to underclaiming of social assistance benefits.[3] The emphasis on reducing fraudulent claiming of benefits has acted to discourage many claimants from seeing even regulated benefits – to which they have a legal right – as entitlements. These perceptions can be encouraged by the treatment of claimants by some social security officials, who have often operated implicit or explicit systems of classifying claimants into 'undeserving' and 'deserving' groups.[4]

Many claimants shared the common perception that (in particular) being unemployed or, more generally, on benefit, meant that they were intrinsically of less value than others in society. Melanie, a lone parent, spoke for many: 'when you're on the scrapheap, you're scrap'. Similarly, a long-term unemployed man living in an area of high unemployment, and who could not get a job with a wage adequate to support his family, reflected:

> I don't like living off the state the way I am. I'd rather have a job, I would . . . and the kids cop it because other kids say your dad's living off the state and all the rest of it, the taxpayers are paying your dinners.

The general impression from both studies was that claimants often shared the negative attitudes to being on benefit held by others who were in work – a reflection of the wider regard with which society was encouraged to view the values of self-reliance and economic independence. One mother commented:

> when I go down to the office with my husband, I feel like something that's crawled out from under a stone. From the attitude of the officials, you'd think it was their money . . .

Claimants' comments often reflected not only the more general view that being a claimant was a position of inferior status, but also the widely-held but contradictory perception that living on benefit was in some way comfortable. Sandra summed up one aspect of this paradox eloquently:

> They've got to lose the idea that people love living on social security

. . . It seems the assumption is that if people are comfortable on the money you're giving them, they're not going to make an effort to get any better – which is kind of insulting really . . . Most people have got a certain amount of pride until it's kicked out of them . . . It feels to me that they have this idea that if people have really got to struggle on it, they'll go out and . . . do something to get themselves out this hole – as if what you're doing is self-inflicted. It seems to be a guilt thing – make them feel guilty and they'll go out and do more for themselves.

For some, the drive to get off benefit as a result of these feelings was considerable, whatever the realities of their situation. Lila, the mother of one family living on benefit, reflected that:

We don't always want to live on the state if we can avoid it . . . that's what it feels like.

Yet her husband was sick and unable to work, she was pregnant, and they had a disturbed older daughter for whom they received attendance allowance. There was no suitable care provision in the area for any of their children.

As a result of such tensions, for many claimants being on benefit remains a distressing and degrading experience, especially at the level of ordinary community life. Lila and Cyril were an active church-going couple but Cyril admitted that:

you feel . . . a bit humiliated by not (being) able to achieve the things that . . . not luxury, but things that are essential, that we really need and you can't have it because of financial difficulties . . . We don't go out of our way to tell people we're on benefit.

Asian families also reflected a strong cultural and religious preference for being able to work. A mother remarked:

We don't feel good about it . . . there's more goodness in working with your own hands. But the problem is he can't get work . . . He used to work even for a low wage but now there isn't any work for him. No doubt those in work say 'oh, they're claiming' but what can we do?

In fact her husband and many like him could do very little to find even low-wage employment. The Pakistani communities in Bradford and the Midlands had been adversely affected by the impact of restructuring, merger and closures within the textiles and engineering industries and the consequent loss of thousands of unskilled and semi-skilled jobs.

'Feeling like a beggar' because of the interaction of their own cultural views and their perceptions of how they were treated by social security officials was likely particularly to discourage more orthodox Muslim claimants. As one put it:

> Begging is like a permanent bruise which will not go away. It brands you, and is a very demoralising thing to say about someone.

Overwhelmingly, then, the impression conveyed by claimants' comments was of their incorporation of a view of claimants as second-class citizens. This took no account of how far their situation was in any way within their control.

STIGMA AND BEING STIGMATISED

Many of the claimants expressed feelings of stigma derived from their experience of the social security system, and of their daily social contacts; feelings which had become more or less internalised. They felt stigmatised by others but also the stigma of their position.

The experience of one older mother with disabilities reflected how the social security system incorporated this wider emphasis within society on getting work. Her own physical disability limited the scope of work she was able to undertake. Nevertheless, she generally felt degraded by 'having to count pennies' and felt that 'people are kept in their place by poverty'. She had applied for help from the social fund, felt embarrassed by the visitor looking round her home and said that applying for one-off payments was 'like begging'. Now that her son was 16 and had left school:

> ... I've had trouble from the DSS ... they're asking me to fill in forms about why can't you get a job. But all the young men round here are out of work. I've worked all my life apart from when I hurt my back, so why are they on at me? They've had information from my GP but they still keep sending me forms. I feel trapped ... Their priorities are all wrong ... instead of chasing people like me, they should find jobs for the young ones.

The emphasis on feeling 'like a beggar' was not unusual and derived in part from the experience of claiming. A couple with three children 'felt awful' about wearing second-hand clothes and borrowing from friends, but they had given up hope of getting help from 'the social'. The mother remarked:

> It's about time they sorted themselves out . . . You have to go and beg for money and you shouldn't have to. They're supposed to be there to help us, not to pull us down. I don't like going to them because it's like begging.

DIFFERENT RACE, DIFFERENT TREATMENT?

It was clear from the comments of some Asian claimants that, notwithstanding their own problems of communication in the English language, they felt they were treated differently by social security officials because they were Asian. Within a particularly tightly-knit Muslim community such as the one in West Bradford, such experiences were reported and shared. The father of five children observed:

> If you are black, you feel it, perhaps more . . . some officials are okay. Some pull their faces now and then. It hurts but you accept it and ignore it.

Despite this experience, they felt that the system generally helped people, although it was in need of improvements. This sense of being treated differently, often in subtle ways, was clear from other claimants' views. In the words of another mother with five children:

> There is no doubt that they don't look well on us people and that is why it takes so long to get an answer from them, or when it's late they take even longer. It's more difficult if you don't know the language or can't read or write English.

One lone parent with a dependent elderly mother and a child with disabilities was sure that being Asian affected her chances of getting extra help:

> Being Asian has affected me because other blind people get extra benefits and my daughter doesn't. I don't understand it . . . I have applied many times but they say no you can't have it. If I was a white person they would give it.

Others, such as this father of three, had no direct experience of racism himself but was aware of it being a problem more generally for Asian claimants:

> There are no doubt problems because these people don't look too well upon our people but till now I haven't experienced it myself. But then I don't really go there much [to the social security office] and if I do, I go with somebody because of the English.

In a few cases, structural racism affected how Asian claimants were treated. Tahira, an immigration 'widow', had good English and a professional work background. She was (wrongly) refused income support in her own right when unemployed and pregnant because the DSS insisted she was part of a couple. In fact her husband remained in Pakistan pursuing an immigration appeal to enter the UK. Three other Asian lone parents appeared to be substantially underpaid because the DSS had (also wrongly) split benefit between them and their separated partners. None of the three was aware that this was being done.

DEALING WITH THE SYSTEM

Claimants emphasised that they found direct dealings with the DSS difficult and stressful, especially if they had to call at the office – often having to wait hours to be seen – rather than telephone. The atmosphere of the waiting rooms – with, sometimes, drunk, rowdy or aggressive people also waiting – discouraged many of them from going there. Although several claimants reported helpful experiences with officials, including social fund officers, these were substantially outweighed by reports of unhelpful staff attitudes: 'you're just a number on a piece of paper' or 'they're a law unto themselves.' Lila's experience was typical:

> They don't inform you of anything if you go down there. If they was to say well, it'll be taken off and we'll do this or we'll do that, they don't actually sit down, they're not willing to explain anything to you, they don't explain your rights or anything else. I mean you can sit down there all day and it depends who you get. You could go up to the desk, or you could go up and (see) somebody that just can't be bothered and then you get annoyed . . . It's oh, fill in a form and

we'll let you know and then you fill in a form and nobody ever acknowledges that form, you've got to go back and say have you had my form? . . . You're in limbo.

There was also little overall indication that the long-standing and well-reported feelings of alienation and suspicion between staff and claimants had been reduced by recent changes in procedure:

Some officials are okay but some act as if you're begging . . . They must be terrified of us all with all those screens up in the office.

Many claimants continued to believe that they were under constant suspicion of trying to 'work the system'. For example, one woman with disabilities was told by an official that 'anyone can put a calliper on a leg to avoid having to register for work.' Conversely, some claimants also suspected that, although mistakes were sometimes genuine, officials were generally trying to offer as little as necessary to keep them quiet.

Lone Asian women, particularly orthodox Muslim women who had had a dependent economic role prior to the death of or separation from a spouse, were liable to find dealing with social security officials even more difficult. This was the result of both problems with language and the fact that their social role did not normally involve them in having to deal with outside authorities.

Some claimants, as noted earlier, because of their lack of understanding of the premium system, were not receiving the more unusual premiums to which they were entitled such as disabled child premium. Lila and Cyril Malleson were not getting this premium for their daughter who received attendance allowance. They later claimed it as a result of getting a leaflet, but experienced enormous difficulties having it backdated:

They backdated it and they didn't want to. I had a terrible struggle to get it off them, but kept phoning up every single week, I phoned up the manager, I went down there and shouted at them because they refused to pay it out, they said I wasn't entitled to it. In the end, we sat down there, didn't we Cyril, we sat down there from 9 in the morning till 4 in the evening . . . and then the manageress came out and she apologised and said they were sorry and they backdated it, but I'm sure they still owe me some.

FLEXIBLE AND RESPONSIVE TO NEED?

Many claimants in both studies suffered from benefit maladminis-tration. The most common problems were unreasonable delays, incorrect payments, and administrative difficulties resulting from crises or changes in circumstances, to which the system was supposed to respond speedily and flexibly but often appeared not to be able to do. As we have noted, many claimants also expressed views about the operation of the social fund which confirmed those reported in other studies. They complained of arbitrariness, inflexibility and discrimination between different claimant groups.[5] For example, in the first set of FSU interviews, about one-third of claimants had had benefit order books or giros delayed on more than one occasion. Some said it happened routinely and the delays varied from a few days to two, three or even four weeks. For those with complicated benefits, delays could be considerable. One family with extensive disability-related needs, and in receipt of attendance allowance and severe disablement allowance, had:

> ... a lot of waiting around to hear about things. You don't know where you are, waiting to hear doctors' decisions and so on. I was two months' delay in getting income support. I had to cut back, I wasn't kept informed at all.

Even when their situation was desperate, claimants had little success in getting emergency payments from the DSS when benefit was delayed. For example, a woman with a new baby and no money for two weeks was refused a counter payment until a social worker intervened. The likelihood of delays led to feelings of uncertainty: 'The worst thing is waiting for the cheque to arrive.' With money so tight, even a brief delay could cause a crisis and it was common for people to be pushed into borrowing from family or friends to get by (see Chapter 3).

The routine payment of income support – two weeks in arrears for new claimants – itself precipitates very many 'crises' which the social fund is supposed to deal with. As the interviews conducted for these studies and other reports[6] demonstrate, the consequences of taking out a crisis loan often linger on, affecting claimants' ability to cope with already low levels of benefit. For example, Mr Bould applied for a crisis loan when he and his girlfriend separated and changed their income support claim. There was a two and a half week delay in benefit being paid and he was obliged to accept a crisis loan of £14, repayable over three weeks (see Chapter 2).

For a number of claimants, the experience of a crisis left them wondering what they would have to do to convince officials of their desperate plight. One lone parent with a baby was burgled and her child benefit and income support order books were stolen, leaving her penniless:

> Eventually I got some money – because they didn't believe me at first, it were awful . . . I says, what am I going to do? I said, I've got nothing, no money. How am I going to feed David?

Some claimants starting families, or with new babies, reported difficulties with getting child benefit. Often payments were delayed for months because of the income support/child benefit interface. Two lone parents interviewed in the FSU study were finally able to get large child benefit arrears paid, but only through the intervention of advice centre workers. One Bradford family waited a year for child benefit. Their forms were lost several times and the gas board 'came to cut us off because of arrears. They didn't know we were on [fuel] direct . . . '

Claimants also found that the social security system often did not respond quickly or appropriately in the face of changing circumstances. Other recent studies have shown that the social fund in particular is increasingly dominated by demands for extra help precisely at the point at which claimants' circumstances change significantly – for example, in moving house, losing a job, having a baby, leaving an institution, or separating from a partner. In the FSU study, two unemployed men found their benefit payments totally disrupted when they went off income support and on to Employment Training (ET) schemes. One left ET as a result. Three women had arguments with DSS benefit officials about their entitlements when it was suggested (wrongly) that they were cohabiting.

CONCLUSION

Despite the structural changes in benefit in 1988, intended in part to make the system simpler, and additional administrative changes, many claimants still experienced the social security system as intrusive, slow-moving, often inaccurate and, at times, punitive.

Financial pressure for claimants, combined with difficulties for staff (many of whom were also low-paid, working under considerable stress and coping with the impact of major organisational changes), too often led to feelings of hostility, arguments and even, in a very few cases, physical fights. It is hardly surprising that scapegoating of 'unpopular' claimant groups was a not uncommon response from both staff and claimants, particularly where feelings of 'having done your bit for the country' were involved. One such pensioner remarked 'we're the worst-off pensioners in Europe: we've been sold out by this country, the immigrants get so much.'

Given their general lack of understanding of how the system works and how benefits are calculated, difficulties highlighted for Asian claimants (particularly where their grasp of spoken or written English was less than colloquial), many claimants perceived the social security office as, at best, unhelpful and unsupportive and, at worst, downright hostile. One lone parent remarked with feeling: 'social security makes my life difficult, as if hell is here'.

Few claimants said they would turn to social security for help in an emergency. Some actively expressed a positive preference for going to 'loan sharks'. Virtually no Asian households said they would use social security in emergencies, preferring for both 'pull' (cultural) and 'push' (social security office regime) reasons to turn to family and friends for help, despite the loss of social status which this sometimes entailed. Similarly, only a handful of claimants said they would turn to social security for money advice or help with sorting out debts.

Rather than offering the possibility of independence and choice, the most common feelings produced by the claiming process were those of powerlessness and mystification. The giro comes and the claimant accepts it – or it doesn't, in which case the claimant, or someone who feels more competent, or speaks better English, rings the office and starts the difficult process of 'staking their claim'.

REFERENCES

1   Greater London Citizens' Advice Bureaux 1986, *Out of Service*, GLCAB, London; Moodie, M, et al, 1988, *The Business of Service*, DHSS, London; National Audit Office, 1991, *The Social Fund*, NAO, HC190, London.

2   Gordon, P and Newnham, A, 1985, *Passport to Benefits: Racism in social security*, CPAG, London; National Association of Citizens' Advice Bureaux, 1991, *Barriers to Benefit*, NACAB, London.

3   Bradshaw, J, 1985, 'Tried and Found Wanting' in Ward, S (ed), *DHSS in Crisis*, CPAG, London, pp102–111.

4   Cooper, S, 1984, *Observations in Supplementary Benefit Offices*, Policy Studies Institute, London; Howe, LEA, 1985, 'The deserving and the undeserving: practice in an urban local social security office', *Journal of Social Policy*, Vol.14, Part 1, Cambridge, pp49–72.

5   Craig, G (ed), 1989, *Your Flexible Friend?*, Social Security Consortium/ Association of Metropolitan Authorities, London; Craig, G, and Coxall, J, (eds), 1989, *Monitoring the Social Fund*, Department of Applied Social Studies, University of Bradford, Bradford; Becker, S, and Silburn, R, 1990, *The New Poor Clients*, Nottingham Benefits Research Unit/Community Care, Nottingham; Social Security Research Consortium, 1991, *Cash limited: limited cash*, Association of Metropolitan Authorities, London.

6   Social Security Research Consortium, 1991, *See* note 5.

5 Poor relations

It's a very depressing thought to think we might have to spend maybe the next five years on social security ... It's a very disheartening, depressing thought, to bring your new baby into the world, because when I had him, do you know one of my first thoughts was 'Isn't he beautiful ... oh I'm so happy, oh God, how am I going to manage to bring him up and keep him fed and clothed decently?' That sums it up for me.

Lorraine Shorter

In this chapter we look at how living on benefit affected claimants' general well-being and that of their families. This includes examining the impact of poverty on how claimants felt, how their poverty affected family relationships and to what degree it limited their ability to take part in social and community activities.

For many, worrying about money clearly led directly to stress and anxiety, which were also sometimes reflected in stress-related health problems. In addition, for some people it produced feelings of general demoralisation and depression. Most felt excluded by lack of money from many normal experiences and activities. This lack of external stimulus compounded the other stresses and strains of being poor to make people feel, in varying degrees, bored, isolated and powerless. Relationships with those closest to them were often, inevitably, affected. Parents suffered a double blow: not only did they feel deprived themselves, but they were forced to watch their children being deprived of things that other children possessed. All too often they felt guilty, that they were not being good parents; that the solution was out of their control.

PERSONAL WELL-BEING

STRESS AND WORRY

The struggle to survive and balance the budget (see Chapter 3) was a real source of worry and stress for most of the people with whom we talked. For many, just managing from day to day and stretching out the weekly money was an anxiety which dominated their life. As Mrs Austin said: 'you worry every week wondering if you're going to have enough.'

As many people explained graphically, working out how to cover bills or other lump sums could worsen the strain. For example, Sandra, like other mothers with fast-growing children, dreaded them needing new clothes:

> If someone puts something on and says 'Mummy, this is getting too tight', you think 'Oh no!' Straight away your heart's in your boots.

Sandra also described the feelings aroused by bills:

> As soon as the bills come my blood pressure's up . . . As soon as it comes through the letterbox . . . and sometimes I can't open it then and there because I just haven't got the strength, the emotional strength, to open it and see what the amount is. I have to put the letter up and wait until I feel mentally I can face looking at it.

FEELING TRAPPED?

The restrictions associated with lack of money make people feel trapped. As Neil and Lorraine explain their situation and describe their feelings, the vicious circle becomes apparent: no money leads to a lack of confidence and possible apathy.

[Neil]

> I think the real problem of being on the dole is it destroys your self-esteem, you know, and your ability to provide for yourself . . . I feel a great lack of self-esteem and I think I'd really like to have a job where I could go out and come back and Lorraine as well could go out . . . Where we could go out and earn some money and have a sense of achievement at the end of the day . . .

I said lack of self-esteem but I mean also, like, a lot of apathy. If you're on the dole for a long period of time you tend to get – well, I tend to get – quite apathetic in many ways. Some weeks, you know, I'll have a lot of energy and I think, Oh, I'll go and do this and I'll try and see if I can get a job here or a job there, and other weeks –

[Lorraine]

That's usually, though, when we've got a giro and we've got a bit of money and there's a bit of food in the cupboard . . . we both tend to change our whole, you know, [attitude], even with the kids we're much more patient . . .

[Neil]

When the money is tighter I suppose we do become a bit more withdrawn and when you've got a bit of money in your pocket you feel a lot more optimistic, I think . . . And therefore you feel like going out, and not just going out and spending money, but going out and doing other things. 'I've got money in my pocket, I've got security, I've got something to fall back on, therefore I can go out and do whatever.' But when it's really tight – you'd think that would have the opposite effect, when you've got no money you'd think that would drive you to go out and look for work, but I've found out that's not always the case . . .

. . . When you go into the post office [to collect the fortnightly giro] and there's a big lump sum . . . [you feel] much more optimistic about the world, you know, looking at the world through rose-tinted glasses.

Sandra expressed similarly powerful feelings:

It's hard to explain. I feel that everything in life is on a downward spiral at the moment, I can't see anything to be really hopeful about . . . I used to have dreams about the future; I don't care to think about the future too much. I still try to hope.

Anjum's sense of incarceration was linked to feelings of inadequacy about providing for her children:

Sometimes they carry on a lot, especially the little one . . . [when they go out] if their mother is with them you can be sure they will be asking, they don't always think about if there is anything in mother's pocket or not. Then my heart feels sad and depressed and so I don't feel like taking them anywhere either.

Lack of mobility increased isolation – a 76-year-old pensioner described the frustration of 'not being able to get out anywhere or see anyone.' Since the Freedom Ride (a service which picked up elderly and disabled people from their doors and took them to shops in town) had been cut, she could not afford to take a taxi into town but found the local shops too expensive:

> I can't use the buses, I'd have to walk too far.

Those whose overall morale seemed relatively high usually based their optimism on getting off benefit. For example, describing how she had to buy everything second hand, a lone parent declared:

> I'm not ashamed to say it, I don't care, because I know that I'm not going to be in poverty for the rest of my life, because I'm determined not to be. Because I used to cry and all that but I don't no more because I hold up my head . . . I want something for myself . . .

THE 'GOOD PARENT' BIND

Andrew and Christine Downing spoke for many others when they said that the worst thing about being on social security was 'watching the children go without'. Shortage of money had a special impact on the self-esteem of parents. They often saw being a good parent as of overriding value and this was usually judged at least in part by how much they could give to the children in material terms. It was intensely distressing when they could not afford to give the children what they felt they needed. Sandra explained it this way:

> I have actually had to swallow my pride till it hurts . . . It makes me feel like a complete failure because I had such high ideals . . . I wanted to give my children the best, not to the point of spoiling them, but just so they could, you know, have confidence in themselves. So when I can't do that it makes me feel I'm failing.

It may be easy for better-off parents to dismiss the material side of parenting but the claimants we interviewed could not do so, however much they wanted to. Many mentioned feeling 'awful', feeling 'guilty' about having to say no to the children; like Sandra, they felt they had failed in some way. Typical comments were:

> I can't buy enough things. It makes me desperate because I can't do anything about it.

Kids understand I can't afford things but I still feel awful.

Money shows you care, you don't have to prove yourself as much.

External pressures also played a part. Many were like the lone parent who said:

I don't want my kids to suffer because I'm on the social . . . I feel awful when other kids' dads are working.

Parents did not want their children to be singled out at school or by their friends because they did not have the right clothes or could not afford school trips. There was often a direct conflict between trying as far as possible to balance the budget and trying to fulfil the children's desires. For example, Marie and Jim Denton were struggling to reduce large debts, but they reluctantly took out a 'Provident' loan, trapping them still further into debt:

. . . to put clothes on the children's backs, for going to school . . . I didn't want them to have the embarrassment of going out the door with their old clothes on and getting ribbed about it.

Whatever the decision in these circumstances, the parent would be left feeling bad. Despite her best endeavours, Sandra, for example, still felt guilty:

[describing when she had to feed the family on sandwiches for a week to pay a big electricity bill] . . . I just get the kids together and say, well, I'm sorry but this has happened. I'm afraid there'll be no dinners this week . . . I'm sort of getting used to doing that now but I still feel, God, you know, I'm not fulfilling my role as a mother properly here.

PRESSURES ON WOMEN

Women were more likely than men to associate their own sense of self-worth with how they provided for and brought up the children. In some cases, this identification was absolute. Some mothers' self-sacrifice in the quest to be 'good mothers' while lacking material resources led them to submerge their own physical and mental needs. As Anjum said:

My own needs are not so important but through them [children] my needs are fulfilled.

As shown in Chapter 3, this led some to cut back on eating properly.

Lone mothers often seemed under great pressure of this kind. It could be accentuated where, for example, they had escaped from a damaging relationship and now felt more in control of their lives and their finances – but then felt even more driven to show they could be 'good parents'. This determination in the face of inadequate finances meant that their goal was often achieved only at great personal cost.

The following are typical comments:

> With all the children's needs going on I don't even have time to think about myself . . . I never think about myself, the children are always first.

> I make sure the children eat first; if there's any left I will. If not . . . then it doesn't matter about me.

> It's more difficult with a baby . . . I don't spend on myself any more.

RELATIONSHIPS WITHIN THE FAMILY

COUPLES

A number of couples said that lack of money created tensions. The daily strain of having to cope on inadequate benefit combined with feelings of being on top of each other at home, without much social contact, to cause arguments between partners. Andrew Downing graphically explained the pressures:

> You end up pulling your hair out because you can't ever get away for a night out like working people . . . Tensions build when you can't get a bit of time on your own.

When these pressures are not released socially, they can get turned inwards:

> When people call for a drink we can't go . . . I feel embarrassed to go with relations in case they think we're sponging . . . then we row with each other.

A younger woman commented:

> After I've had one night out I'm stuck in the flat for a week on my own . . . I argue with him (boyfriend) over cigarettes and food, who's eaten the last tin of soup.

The pressures of poverty exerted stress on even the strongest relationship.

RELATIONSHIPS WITH CHILDREN

Such tensions were often compounded by feelings of frustration at having to say 'no' to the children – and when they too felt they were missing out, conflicts developed. These were depressing for everyone. As one mother described:

> The children are always asking for things, they say their friends have this and this . . . we have to say no, so the children get upset and we feel upset.

In some cases, this tension seemed to be linked with emotional/behavioural problems in children. One lone parent explained:

> If I haven't got any money for sweets the oldest kid he starts to swear and act up . . . [I] had to put him under a care unit.

The boy had also developed asthma. His mother worried about him which in turn affected her health. 'I worry a lot, I'm bad with my nerves.' Another lone parent reported the effects of money worries on her relationship with her children:

> I'm very short with them, especially when it's can we have, can we have, all the time . . .

There could be an extra turn of the screw when parents had separated, leaving the caring parent – almost invariably, among the people we saw, the mother – dependent on benefit. Sometimes the inevitable upset and adjustment associated with the departure of the father were exacerbated by a drop in income. Conflicts with children over money did not usually occur in families with pre-school children, who were too young to realise what they were missing. However, older children could blame their mother for the fact that there was not enough money. One mother explained how her 14-year-old daughter reproached her:

> She's just saying that since daddy went you've been more and more like this. Since he's gone you've been doing this too much, saying we haven't got the money.

SOCIAL AND COMMUNITY ACTIVITIES

EXCLUDING THE CHILDREN

As already noted, claimants commonly described the experience of exclusion from activities which others could take for granted. Adults were especially concerned about this for their children. Many of the children had to miss out on things that children with working parents regarded as unexceptional. For example, most did not get away on holiday. In the FSU study, only one or two families managed holidays, although some children did go away with the school or through FSU. Over 75 per cent of the families interviewed in Bradford did not have a regular annual week's holiday away. Children often had to miss out on school trips and outings with their friends:

> We can't afford to send the children on school trips, so they stay home for the day.

A lone parent explained:

> There's no extras, I can't afford to go with friends' families to McDonald's for tea.

A father echoed this:

> The oldest, he likes ice-skating . . . but we can't afford to let him go.

Parents found it especially hard to see their children excluded at times of celebration and festivals when their limited income would just not stretch to any substantial extra expense. In this situation they would either have to sacrifice something else or say no. Andrew expressed the bitterness many felt when he said that Christmas was 'a joke'. Lorraine Shorter viewed this 'celebration' with dread:

> We've got Christmas coming up . . . For me that's not any enjoyment, it's a nightmare. I look in the shops, looking at prices and it's a bloody nightmare.

Life could be even more difficult for Asian parents who often found themselves faced with budgeting for some of the celebrations and customs of both the Pakistani and British cultures. While for other parents giving the children a good Christmas was a priority, the Asian parents' equivalent concern was the struggle to keep up with

MAGGIE MURRAY/FORMAT

'I don't think about anything except the money and how to stretch it.'

the normal expectation of new clothes for the Eid festival. Mohammed Azam described the difficulties:

> For special occasions like Eid, if they [children] have things that will do then I won't buy anything else, they just have to wear the old ones. It does hurt that you can't clothe your children, not even on special days . . . but what can you do?

With these competing demands, sometimes one festival had to be ignored to pay for others. An Asian mother explained:

> Not much is done towards birthdays, the children are used to not celebrating that.

In fact, children's birthdays were a particularly painful issue, as one mother – faced with sudden financial demands when a council flat came up – described:

> It was her birthday on Saturday and because we moved we couldn't buy her anything, not even a cake . . . Luckily she's too young to understand at the moment, but . . . this Christmas I've had to explain to my older girl – she wants an organ – I've had to explain 'you won't get it this year' which she's upset about, because . . . to her, although it's nice to move, it's not a Christmas present.

A lone mother's dilemma was even more acute:

> My eldest daughter [aged 14] has been saying that she wants to celebrate her birthday . . . she's been crying all the time . . . She's saying she's going to have a birthday party but I'm saying no. I said to her 'you invite all those people, and they can come and sit on the sofa, but I won't be making anything' . . . I just haven't got the money.

ADULT SOCIAL LIFE

Like the children, adults often found their social life severely limited. In general, people had very little money to socialise with friends and were therefore often deprived of much social contact outside the home. The exceptions were people who clearly had a strong network of local friends and/or family – often themselves on benefit – whom they saw regularly and with whom they provided mutual support. In a few cases, relations would pay for them to participate in outings.

Without such help, it was difficult to get out and take part in social events. Only four out of 30 two-parent families in Bradford stated that they regularly had any spending money left at the end of the week. The other 26 couples and all 22 lone parents stated that they never or only occasionally had money left. A similar picture was painted by the FSU families. The following comments are typical:

> We haven't had a night out for years.

> I'd like to be able to go out now and again but I've no money left on Friday when friends call.

People complained that they did not have enough money even to do ordinary things like inviting friends round for a meal:

> It's very shameful when you can't treat your guests good and feed them well . . . The government only gives a little bit of money which isn't even enough to feed yourself, let alone anyone else that comes to the house.

Lone parents had the additional problem of coping with children on their own, with little or no access to childcare facilities:

> I meet my friend on a Tuesday . . . and we have a little walk round town . . . But no, normally I hardly get any visitors at all. I get fed up . . . It does get lonely because when Andrew [child] is in bed, that's it, I'm on my own . . . It's just that sometimes I'd like to drop every-thing, you know, and go out and just let my hair down sort of thing . . . I'm young, you know, I'm 21, and if I'm not going out and enjoy-ing myself I'll never meet anybody, will I? Because one day I'd like to meet somebody and settle down . . . I'd like to, you know, meet Mr Right and maybe get married.

In the few couples who had a little spare money, it was generally the husband who spent this on his own entertainment. Yet these men by no means had what the majority of the population would consider access to an acceptable social life. One father commented:

> If there is some money left I go out with my friends, but even then I feel ashamed because you need quite a bit to go out.

This feeling of inadequacy could be reinforced by being excluded from other social experiences for which money was necessary. For example, one lone parent explained how she dreaded social occasions with her family because she hated the way they made her feel:

> [like] Cinderella at the ball . . . I don't talk much, they all talk about material things.

Childless people also found themselves excluded. Most pensioners, even if they were mobile, said they were unable to afford an evening out:

> They [friends] say come out for the night and offer to pay for me, but I won't go – wouldn't sponge off anyone.

Young people could also feel isolated. One young woman summed up the effect of poverty on her relationship with the outside world:

> Your quality of life is different when you're not working. Being on benefit forces you into a ghetto. You've no freedom to buy a newspaper or have a meal out.

SOCIAL OBLIGATIONS

Lack of money could make it difficult or impossible to keep up with social obligations which others take for granted. Lorraine Shorter talked about the quandary with which she and Neil were faced when they did not have the money to buy even a small present for their 6-year-old daughter Anna to take to a neighbouring child's birthday party. Andrew Downing described a similar dilemma:

> The telly broke down and I got my mate's dad to fix it as a favour to me. I felt awful – the bloke's done me a favour and I can't even say 'here's a couple of quid, get yourself a drink'.

Many Asian families found it difficult or impossible to keep up with the traditional 'give and take' gift-giving on special occasions (such as weddings) which is practiced in the Muslim Pakistani culture. Because of financial pressure, some families who could not afford it opted out of 'the give and take' or reduced their participation, which could lead to them feeling more isolated than before. Asked if she kept up with the 'give and take', Anjum explained:

> Only with the close important ones, you know, we have to do that, to give to brothers and sister. Like at weddings we have to give suits and

it's a real struggle because people will say 'Oh, so and so has only given this much . . . ' But what can you do about it when you just don't have the money? We just give what we can, but it's a pressure because it's so important.

Mohammed Azam elaborated on the pressures felt by Muslim families:

There are some places where you can't just say no . . . especially where it is family. You have to keep face because we have to live with these people . . . and also if we give now then when it's our turn then they will give us; that's what this giving and taking is about, isn't it? . . . It's not that we give a lot, anyway, we give the least amount . . . and even that is with so much difficulty, but we do it out of desperation, just to keep up the relationship with people.

Some people in the FSU study played an active part in helping to run services at the local FSU Unit, and several were involved with the local church, which provided an important social outlet for them.

But lack of money could have an effect even on church-going. In Chapter 2, Sandra described how she was unable to afford to take all the children to church and also her problems in keeping up with other organisations.

I'm a member of the Church council and a governor of the [primary] school. Those things I've kept up. I was on the PTA at St Joseph's [secondary school]. I've dropped that and I've dropped the tenants' association. I gave them up because at the time I had no one to look after the children. And I did get to the point where I had no clothes to wear to go . . . [and] . . . Oh yes, how could I go to those meetings in trainers with no soles, and jeans with holes in?

QUALITY OF LIFE: POWER, CONTROL AND CHOICE

Permeating the conversations we had with these claimants was the sense that they found their choices in many areas of their lives severely limited and felt, to varying degrees, a general lack of power and control. This theme recurred when discussing other aspects of poverty, and has been covered earlier in this chapter and elsewhere in the book (see Chapters 3 and 4).

LACK OF POWER

Especially for people on benefit long-term, lack of money meant having to battle to maintain control. Sandra described the worst thing about being on social security as:

> . . . not being able to keep up my standards . . . You never get a firm hold on life, you feel life's doing things to you. You're not in control, life is really biffing you about . . . It's a frightening thing . . . I like to be in charge of my life and my children's lives and in control of what's happening to us . . .

Discussing how the money was buying less and less as prices went up, she added:

> . . . until a few years ago I felt I had a tentative grip on what was happening to us, but not now.

Sandra's feelings were echoed by other claimants, who spoke often of being 'forced', or 'desperate', or asked 'what can we do?' Choices were often seen as illusory – for example, one claimant asked bitterly 'will we eat or pay poll tax?' This feeling of powerlessness under-pinned much of the stress and demoralisation already described.

An interchange between a couple makes the distinction between 'living' – not being on benefit – and 'existing' – their life on income support.

[Father]

> We're not living on the dole, we're just existing barely.

[Mother]

> That's what it is, an existence.

[Question]

> [So what's the difference between existing and living?]

[Father]

> Living is where I could go into a shop and say I'll have a pound of steak, my bairns fancy a bit of steak. I'd like a pair of shoes, fit them on my bairn and I'll take them.

[Mother]

> Existing is just going into a shop and saying give us half a pound of chopped pork, for my five bairns, my wife and myself.

Lorraine Shorter complained:

> There's no choice, you never get a choice. I hate being on the social!

This was a common theme. People had little choice over everyday decisions, such as what they eat and wear. This could have psychological effects, making them feel powerless and degraded. In the Bradford study, almost two-thirds of the non-Asian families could not afford to buy any of their clothes new. Most found being forced to continually buy second-hand clothes particularly frustrating. A father of four explained:

> We had to use them. You had to line up and know what you were going for and then be disappointed when it wasn't there, you had no freedom.

Parents often could not afford to buy their children clothes when they needed them. Two mothers' comments, expressed in almost identical terms, were typical:

> I'd like to be able to afford to buy them clothes without having to juggle and make them plod on but I have no choice.

> I feel awful about wearing other people's clothes but I have no choice.

This was felt even more keenly where there was some special need involved. A mother with a handicapped son who wore out his clothes and sheets quickly had to rely on her family for 'cast-offs' as she could not afford to keep up with his clothing needs:

> I don't like it but we've got to make do and mend, haven't we?

Sandra described a recurrent dream which poignantly illustrated her lack of choice:

> I dream about finding the back door of Marks and Spencer open and going in and just picking up all the things that I want – would like – for me and the children. I have nightmares about being at a counter full of children's clothes reduced at ridiculous prices and I'm grabbing all these clothes – this will do for Jenny, this will do for Darren – and then finding I haven't got a purse with me, and I have no money . . .

So that's the one [dream] for the children; but my one is a kind of fantasy and the doors open and I go in and pick up all these beautiful clothes. I have to have what I can afford at the time so I go out some days feeling very depressed about what I'm wearing, because it's not me. It's just not me!

LACK OF VARIETY, SPONTANEITY AND CHOICE

Lack of purchasing power meant that life was monotonous and lacking in variety. This particularly applied to food. Andrew Downing commented that he hated:

> . . . having to live hand to mouth, minute to minute, buying the same stuff [food] every week, eating the same meals every week.

Not eating meat as often as they wanted was one of the most obvious limitations on diet. Two mothers noted:

> You can't really choose to do anything . . . you can't say 'Oh I feel like having some lamb today' because I know I can't afford it.

> We can't always afford fresh meat or veg . . . we have to go without variety.

A lone mother with three children under five reflected both the constant struggle to manage on an inadequate budget and the need to deny her own requirements:

> I've changed diet lots of times to manage . . . You know, cut down on meat [because] it's so expensive.

Lack of money also ruled out spontaneity: claimants could not choose to do something unexpectedly on the spur of the moment which had not been strictly planned and budgeted for. A lone parent illustrated this:

> It would be nice to see things in a shop and go in and buy them there and then instead of next week.

A couple with two children described how they could not afford unbudgeted-for 'extravagances' such as fish and chips:

> One night we felt like a change, that was £6 for supper for the four of us . . . you mustn't (do it) . . . you're just punishing yourself.

Over and over again terms such as 'no freedom' or being 'forced' to do something illustrated the link between shortage of money and feelings of powerlessness. We conclude this chapter with comments which typify the lack of control and choice felt by claimants:

> We had no freedom . . . had to think about everything we bought.

> The money is not enough but there's nothing I can do about it.

> On the whole life is limited. It all revolves around what benefits you get.

> I don't think about anything except the money and how to stretch it.

6 A poor life

I do not want many alterations in the law ... but I should like the best things made free. We want many more baths and wash-houses, especially swimming baths; and they should be free and open in every district. Books and pictures should be freely shown, so that every man may have a public library or a picture gallery in his drawing-room, where he can enjoy what is good with his boys and girls. We want more open space so that every man, woman and child might sit in the open air and see the sky and the sunset ... we want free provision of the best forms of pleasure ... Poverty cannot pay for the pleasure which satisfies, and yet, without that pleasure, the people perish.

(Samuel Barnett in *My Apprenticeship*, Beatrice Webb)

Living on a low income is difficult enough if you are in good health, your home is in good condition and you live in a pleasant area, with access to adequate facilities. However, this was rarely the case among the people interviewed. Lack of money all too often goes along with other kinds of deprivation. This chapter focuses on the interaction between poverty and problems with health, housing and the local environment.

POOR HEALTH

EXTENT OF ILL-HEALTH

Ill-health and disability were common among the people we

interviewed, reflecting the well-established association between poverty and ill-health (see Chapter 1 and Bibliography). This enabled us to examine whether people could meet extra expenses resulting from ill-health and to discover what kind of help they received from the benefit system.

In the FSU study, over 65 per cent (34) of the families reported ill-health or disability among parents, and over 70 per cent (24) among children – most of these conditions being long-term. Similarly, in Bradford, almost two-thirds of the 91 households interviewed reported long-term sickness or disability. In both studies, more than one family member was often affected.

Among children in both studies asthma, bronchitis and eczema were most common – for example, a third of the families in the Bradford study and a quarter in the FSU study reported asthma, and bedwetting was also high on the list in the FSU study. Among the people without children interviewed in Bradford – mainly older people – nearly a third (12) suffered from diabetes, heart disease and/or ulcers. In addition, a wide range of conditions and disabilities was reported among adults and children, including kidney disease, various kinds of back trouble, anaemia, arthritis, depression, blindness, vascular disease, Crohn's disease, sickle cell disease, hernia, epilepsy, learning difficulties, growth problems, and severe behavioural difficulties.

ILL-HEALTH AND STRESS

It seemed that psychological stresses associated with poverty affected health. One lone parent explained it this way:

> When you're down your health goes down. When you know you're worried that's the next stress, because stress causes illness. You'll find a lot of people are sick who's poor because they've got a lot of stresses and if you lift them up a few bob it helps, it really does help.

Just under half (22) of the parents interviewed in Bradford specifically said that money problems led to anxiety which then affected their health. Stress-related health conditions were among those most frequently reported in both research projects (see Chapter 6).

Some people with fluctuating health problems found that a particular financial crisis would immediately have an effect. For example, as described in Chapter 2, this happened to Geoffrey Bould, whose bronchitis became worse when he had specific money worries; similarly, Rashid Chaudry's asthma became worse when he became worried or was not warm enough. A woman in a couple described how it affected her:

> I get moody because I've got no money . . . I end up worrying and then my eczema gets worse.

The effect on ill-health could also be long-term and chronic. A number of women in the FSU study specifically mentioned headaches, loss of weight, and other stress-related illnesses – for example, Sandra developed a bad case of ME. A lone parent with high blood pressure saw the connection very clearly:

> I find I get a lot of headaches and it's all down to stress. It's the situation I'm in . . . I mean it's the money and the situation that everything is my responsibility, you know. I never go out, never get time to relax . . . I think it's stress [that causes] headaches, high blood pressure, all this . . .

EXTRA COSTS – NOT ENOUGH MONEY

In many cases, the illness led to additional expenses for such things as extra clothing or bedding for warmth, special diets, transport costs, extra heating, extra laundry, a phone to contact a GP or hospital in an emergency, or replacing clothing or bedding more often than normal. We found, though, that these costs were usually not met, or not met in full, because there was just not enough money to go round. Where money was found, this was often achieved by cutting back on other necessary expenditure. The pain and stress inevitably associated with ill-health were thus compounded by lack of money, forcing people to live with more discomfort and anxiety than was necessary, or even possibly aggravating their condition.

Here we highlight some of the common areas of difficulty.

DIETS

A typical example was John Forrest, a 60-year-old married man

who had been ill with pernicious anaemia and stomach ulcers for
14 years but who could not afford the special diet prescribed by his
doctor, let alone keep up with his clothing requirements. He and his
wife had to go to second-hand shops for clothes. His wife, Anne,
explained the difficulty of sticking to a special diet:

> The doctor has told him he needs fish and chicken regularly, but we
> can't afford it . . . We seem to live off chips and potatoes . . . [He]
> should have low-fat meat every day, so when we cook anything we
> have to use twice the gas . . . [We] only have a cooked meal three
> times a week to cut down on gas.

Many claimants in both studies said that they could not even afford
what they regarded as a healthy diet, let alone special diets, especially
where these involved cooking separately for one person with the
associated extra fuel costs.

HEATING

Certain illnesses were aggravated by cold or damp, and heating was
often too expensive to avoid such problems. A 45-year-old man
with diabetes and vascular disease was asked what he would spend
an extra £5 per week on:

> Another bag of coal . . . my feet are cold in summer and winter. It
> would help to be able to have more heat.

Parents tended to cut down or turn off the heating during the day,
while the children were out at school, even where they themselves
needed extra heat. One such was a mother with very painful
circulatory problems:

> I just have to sit with a lot of blankets around me and wear warm
> socks. In the winter, you feel like putting on the heating to warm
> them up but then I think about the bill and how I'm going to pay for it
> and I say to myself, leave it. Yes, when the children are here then I will
> put the heater on. They are small so you have to put it on for them,
> don't you?

MULTIPLE HEALTH EXPENSES

Things were even worse where a person or family had a number of extra expenses. A couple in later middle age, who were affected by a number of illnesses including asthma, high blood pressure and ulcers, described the effect of their health problems on their day-to-day living:

> We've had to cut back on heating – the bedroom was like a fridge but we couldn't afford to put the gas heater on, we had to cut down on meat and fish. I ended up very poorly because of not eating the right food . . . I ended up in hospital for a stomach operation.

This also happened in families where several members had health problems. The Denton family is a good example. Two of the four children wet the bed, one has eczema and another asthma; also one of their daughters, who has bowel problems, has been told to follow a high-fibre diet. Jim and Marie are both asthmatic and Marie is allergic to soap powder. Jim has had a serious accident and since then finds he wears down one shoe much more than the other; he now has to buy shoes more often.

The Dentons need to spend more than normal on hot water and washing because the children wet the bed, and also to keep the place warm because of asthma. But with large fuel debts they have to economise:

> Josie . . . was bed-wetting and we couldn't afford to put on the immersion heater for a bath in the morning, so she was having a wash down. But she wasn't washing herself properly so they were getting a smell of urine off her and they were tormenting her about that. So it's a case of now we've got to make sure we've got hot water for her in the morning.

They cannot afford to change Damian's clothes every day, which has been recommended for his eczema, nor to give Josie her high-fibre diet.

TRAVEL AND EMERGENCIES

Some people could not get out and about because of disability and suffered because they could not afford taxis. An 80-year-old extremely frail woman, suffering from a duodenal ulcer, anaemia, chronic bronchitis and severely impaired vision, was practically housebound. Her daughter cared for her, taking washing to the launderette and doing the weekly shopping as well as all the housework. The old lady found making ends meet a struggle. She had no telephone in case of emergencies and no money to pay for taxis to get out at all. She did not even receive attendance allowance and had obviously never thought of claiming it.

Like her, a number of claimants needed a telephone because of health emergencies or to arrange hospital appointments. Melanie Baker's rare form of sickle cell trait led to attacks, as a result of which she had been taken to hospital by ambulance several times. She felt very vulnerable without a phone, with neighbours out all day and with no working public phones nearby. She was only able to get a phone installed when she received a lump-sum payment of child benefit arrears.

Even where neighbours were co-operative, having to depend on them regularly caused difficulties:

> The amount of times we've had to go to neighbours and doctors have had to go to neighbours to phone ambulances or phone hospitals . . . Jeanie [neighbour] is great . . . but I feel it's imposing on her . . . They've got a family of their own . . . and us running in and out and using the phone.

Travel to hospital appointments was also an issue. For some people this involved travelling quite a distance and there was little awareness of their right to have fares refunded: about a third of the people in the FSU study had attended hospital recently but only two had claimed the refund. Two Asian women who could not use public transport because of language difficulties were paying out taxi fares to get to regular appointments.

BENEFITS FOR HEALTH-RELATED EXPENSES

Until 1988, it was possible to get extra help for health-related costs – especially regular extra heating, laundry or diet expenses – through additions to weekly benefit; there were also lump-sum grants for some health-related expenses. But, as we described in Chapter 2, the 1988 changes introduced flat-rate premiums and replaced most one-off grants with loans.

FALLING THROUGH THE NET

Both the studies found that claimants and their families with extra needs caused by disability or ill-health often did not get extra help from income support.

In Bradford, the majority of these claimants were pensioners who had developed their disabilities late in life and who, for some reason, had never applied for benefits to which they may have been entitled. They tended to rely heavily on younger relatives for day-to-day needs such as shopping and cooking, but even with this extra help life was a struggle and over a third of pensioners (five) were only managing at all in this way with considerable difficulty.

In addition, both studies pinpointed difficulties caused by children's ill-health. Under the income support rules, extra money in the form of a disabled child premium is only given if a child gets attendance or mobility allowance. As we have seen, there was a great deal of childhood ill-health among the families interviewed and it often involved extra costs. But typical conditions such as bronchitis or asthma, involving extra heating costs; or eczema, allergies or bedwetting involving extra washing; or kidney trouble involving a special diet – none of these warranted attendance or mobility allowance. So parents with substantial extra costs were receiving no additional help.

A father of four with one asthmatic child who also suffered from a hole in the heart, and another son who was deaf in one ear, felt very disillusioned with the benefits system:

> We put in for a special diet . . . for the youngest . . . he's supposed to be on a low-fat diet . . . but we just got the same thing from the social . . . you're not entitled . . . you don't need it.

LOSING OUT WHEN THE RULES CHANGED

As we discussed in Chapter 2, some people found that their benefit was frozen in 1988 because they were not entitled to so much under the new system. Ironically, this 'freezing' was officially known as transitional *protection*, and often affected people who formerly received extra for health-related expenses.

A lone parent with four children – three asthmatic and two bedwetters – saw it this way: 'they take my heating and my laundry and my bath addition away, so now I only get 90p a week for heating, bath and laundry.' She could not afford to keep her coal-fired central heating going: 'If I can afford coal we have the fire on, if not it just means the kids have got to go to their beds early.'

Even where benefits rose, it was often not enough to keep pace with increasing costs. A 79-year-old woman with heart disease and a crumbling spine had a rise in benefit in 1989. However, she also suffered from incontinence and could not afford to replace her recently broken washing machine. She relies on relatives for gifts of underwear:

> You can't manage because the bills have all gone up . . . I paid my gas yesterday which left me skint. I can't buy clothes . . . I've got nothing left to live on . . . Never mind buying clothes . . . I need new under-clothes but can't afford to buy those . . . I don't get the sort of food I need.

We found few people receiving extra benefits, such as attendance allowance or mobility allowance, especially related to disability – only eight out of the 60 families in Bradford who reported ill-health or disability and four out of the 34 families in the FSU study who did so.

Even those who received these benefits found that they were not always sufficient to cover the extra costs. A middle-aged couple were living on income support and caring for their adult son who had learning difficulties and was incontinent. They were receiving invalidity benefit and attendance allowance, but found that extra benefits did not cover the costs of their son's clothing and bedding:

> We've had to cut back on clothing for ourselves, because we can't cut back on his . . . He needs lots of pyjamas and underwear.

They had to rely heavily on gifts of clothes from relatives and the mother had to make up new sheets from scraps of old ones: 'I don't like it but we've got to make do and mend.'

LOW TAKE-UP OF HEALTH-RELATED BENEFITS

As discussed in Chapter 4, a number of people did not know what benefits they were entitled to or were too proud to claim. An elderly and frail couple (aged 86 and 87 years) had a number of illnesses including heart disease and blindness. Despite being housebound and almost totally dependent on their son for their everyday needs, they received no extra benefits at all. When asked if they had thought about making a special application to the social fund for extra needs, the husband replied: 'We hadn't heard about it. We prefer to manage on our own anyway.'

Both the FSU and the Bradford studies also found low take-up, and particularly a lack of awareness, of the scheme for refund of fares to hospital. We also found that there was considerable ignorance of the rules about the disability premium, especially as these affected couples and lone parents. Where a man was claiming on the basis of sickness and thus submitting medical certificates, the disability premium was, correctly, being paid, although the claimants did not always seem aware of it. But in several couples where the man was claiming as unemployed, the woman appeared to be too ill to work. This would qualify them for the disability premium (a substantial amount extra – almost £24 per week by 1991/92) if the woman were to be the claimant for the couple. But in only one case were they aware of this right. Similarly, there were a number of lone parents who were ill or disabled and could perhaps have been able to get medical certificates showing they were unfit for work, thus entitling them to the disability premium – but again none of them knew about this entitlement.

POOR HOUSING

The immediate home environment is an important aspect of anyone's quality of life. It was especially relevant to these people living on benefit, though, because they spent more time at home than working people. As we have shown, they had little or no money for outings and outside leisure activities.

COLD AND DAMP

More than a third of the people interviewed in both studies said it was difficult or impossible to keep their homes warm and dry. This was often due to structural defects – for example, ill-fitting

'At the moment I'm stuck here. Last week I had two days when I never saw a soul, nobody came, nobody rang, and I can't get out because taxis cost too much.'

doors and windows or ineffective or non-existent damp coursing (see below), but sometimes the fault lay with inadequate heating systems.

A young couple with an 18-month-old child had no heating in damp bedrooms:

> The little one is suffering, it's freezing cold upstairs . . . We can't afford a heater, she's had a cold for the last two months.

Problems with keeping the bedrooms warm caused particular difficulties for larger families. A lone parent with three children had problems with damp in one bedroom and no heating in the upstairs rooms:

> The council won't do anything . . . there's damp in the bedroom, the other one is freezing cold, I've had to move the children out of there.

Even when heating systems were adequate, a simple lack of money to turn up the heating caused problems – exacerbated when the family also could not afford carpets and warm curtains. As discussed above, it was common to economise on heating (over half of the people in the FSU study did so) and in both studies some people with central heating did not use it at all because of shortage of cash. For example, a 75-year-old woman with health problems lived in a specially adapted bungalow and had a perfectly good central heating system. However, she could not afford to turn on her heating till 8.30pm:

> I can't afford to put the central heating on. When the weather is colder I'm shivering. You go out in the rain, come back, and it's not warm enough in the house . . . you go to bed to get warm but if you go to bed cold you can't get warm.

One couple with an 18-month-old baby were on a 'fuel direct' scheme. Despite this, and their attempts to cut down on other expenditure, they still found they were unable to use either the cooker or the hot water as much as they needed to. So they did not cook a hot meal every night, and they bathed the baby in a tub in front of the gas fire.

DISREPAIR

Disrepair was a serious problem on the council estate in Bradford, where many of the houses – especially those occupied by families with children – were in desperate need of improvement. Over half (26) of council tenants reported that ill-fitting, old-fashioned windows with metal frames let in wind and rain, exacerbating heating problems. Over a quarter reported serious damp problems.

Improvements had been delayed due to council spending cuts and many tenants had been waiting months or even years. Problems of 'black' damp in bedrooms and bathrooms seemed widespread and tenants reported a serious lack of co-operation on the part of the council when they reported problems.

A mother of four reported damp problems:

> The bottom floor of the house is damp. The council will do nothing, they say it's condensation.

Almost all the Bradford tenants who reported damp also reported that the council refused to do anything about it. A lone parent with three children, one of whom suffered from asthma, had multiple housing problems including damp, loose windows and a kitchen ceiling which was falling in:

> If water is spilt on the bathroom floor it leaks through to the kitchen, the kitchen ceiling is falling in, the council won't do repairs . . . They say because I did an 'exchange' I'm responsible.

The FSU study suggested that councils and housing associations/ trusts were sometimes cutting back on 'minor' repairs and were inclined to pass the buck to the tenant. This was especially noticeable where several council or housing association tenants moved into newly-built accommodation only to find that repairs immediately needed – for example, because of cracks in the plaster – were not accepted as the landlord's responsibility. Apart from their doubtful legality, such cutbacks caused problems because there was no spare cash for the tenants to buy materials. The extra responsibility could just be an added pressure where someone was already coping with difficulty.

For example, a lone parent who was frail and sometimes unwell, and whose toddler was receiving treatment for growth problems, complained that her flat was draughty and cold, and that there was damp in the bathroom. The council official who inspected the damp was not sympathetic:

> She says 'you'll have to . . . strip the walls yourself and cover it with bleach to seal it and that' . . . Well as if I'm going to do that, because I'm only little! And she said – 'Well, don't you know anybody with ladders?' Anyway luckily my friend's got a ladder, but supposing I fall off the ladder and break my arm or anything, who's going to look after Simon then? So I've got to do it all myself and they're going to give me a £20 decorating grant.

DECORATING

As discussed in Chapter 3, most people found it difficult or impossible to budget for redecoration. For example, over a third (22) of the council tenants interviewed in Bradford said their houses needed decorating. This task was doubly difficult when damp ruined wallpaper and paintwork.

Living on benefit long-term could mean living not just with decoration that needed renewing but also with furniture and furnishings that were inadequate and/or wearing out. Sandra explained the overall effect this could have:

> . . . the house is getting really shabby and that bothers me a lot . . . I always had this overpowering urge to have – not a palace, because you can't have children in a palace . . . but a home they could be proud of, wouldn't be ashamed to bring friends home to. And the standards have gone down, there's no two ways about it, and whereas in the past I would have done something about various things, now I can't; and that really, really bothers me.

PRIVATE BEDSITS AND FLATS

The Bradford study highlighted special problems for private tenants. The standard of decoration and furnishing was generally low, making the immediate surroundings depressing. Furniture and carpets were ill-matched, grimy and worn, electrical appliances were old and usually faulty. However, as three out of four of these tenants lived in bedsits, one of the biggest problems was space. A

49-year-old divorcee described the sheer monotony of living in one room: 'The room is too small, it's bad having to live and sleep in one room.'

Housing association tenants in both studies generally had much better property, although there could still be problems. In Bradford, the (mainly childless) housing association tenants had great difficulty getting furniture and in two cases appeared to have no furniture at all.

LOCAL FACILITIES AND SERVICES

Like housing, local facilities were especially important for the claimants because lack of cash precluded them from having the outings, trips and holidays seen as a normal part of life by their better-off counterparts.

Two types of area were involved in our research. Some people in both studies lived on outlying council estates; others lived in the inner city. In Bradford, the latter were mainly Asian families (but also a few childless people) living within ten minutes' of the city centre. Some families in the FSU study lived in inner neighbourhoods of bigger cities, usually without immediate access to a city centre, others on outlying estates.

DAY-CARE

Lone parents in particular pointed out the need for more local childcare provision – day-care for under-fives, after-school centres and holiday centres. These were either non-existent or very scarce locally. For example, on the Bradford estate there was one nursery with a lengthy waiting list, priority being given to those who worked. Among the families in the FSU study, only four had subsidised or free day-care, usually because of some special family or health problem.

This meant that parents on benefit generally had no relief from the constant company of pre-school children; this could be a real strain, especially for lone parents. Two lone parents felt so desperate that they went short of food and other essentials to pay for nursery places. As one explained:

> I can't have David around me all day – I admit it, I can't cope with
> that . . . it's too much. You're stuck in here all the time, I never go
> out . . . David is on his own, he's got nobody to play with.

Added to this daily frustration was the fact that lone parents could
not go out to work because they could not arrange child-care
facilities. A lone mother with four children said her biggest problem
was 'paying for childcare . . . If I could get a job where I could take
the youngest with me I'd go to work straightaway.'

PLAY FACILITIES

In the FSU study, the most common complaint parents made about
the area was the lack of enough, or suitable, play and other facilities
for children. Lack of play provision was also a problem in Bradford,
although this was less serious for those people on the Bradford estate
who had gardens where children could play safely.

   Specialised play facilities for under-fives and younger children
could be vitally important, especially for lone parents faced with
single-handedly keeping pre-school children amused. In the inner
city area of Bradford, a lone parent living in a top-floor flat reported
that she found it hard to get out. There were not many facilities in
the area for small children. The local playgroup had just closed due
to council cuts:

> It's a bit of a problem getting out through the day. There's not many
> places to take kids her age. If we go out it's usually just for a walk in
> the park.

The lone parent who paid for her three-year-old's nursery place
echoed this; always visiting the same park was not good enough and
there was never any money to vary the routine:

> There's nothing in this area . . . There's nothing outdoors, there's
> nowhere to go, you can't go to the zoo because you can't afford to
> go . . . We go for a walk around the park, yes, every week. Last
> Sunday we went to the park for three or four hours . . . Well, he's not
> interested.

People also complained about lack of facilities for older children, or
that vandalism or insufficient supervision made them unsafe. Marie

Denton, living on an outlying estate, highlighted some of the difficulties:

> You can't go to the adventure playground over there because of the drug users, you can't go over there because of the neighbours, they can't play football in the streets because of the motors, there's nothing left for them . . . I feel rotten that I'm having to ground them for disobeying us, because they only want to play.

The Bradford study also illuminated some of the tensions between generations that could result from inadequate facilities. Young people tended to hang around the local shopping centre or play in the streets. This sometimes caused a disturbance to older, more vulnerable residents who sometimes felt threatened. This situation was made worse by the fact that break-ins were commonplace and almost all householders reported feeling anxious about the possibility of burglary.

LACK OF SAFETY

This leads on to the lack of personal safety felt by some of the people interviewed – especially older people and women.

Break-ins were reported or feared:

> You daren't go out in case of being broken into.

> It's getting worse round here for break-ins and fighting. I don't use the local shops much. Don't feel safe in the area.

A number of women felt unsafe outside the home at night, which in turn could compound other restrictions caused by shortage of money and childcare responsibilities.

Even living in a 'respectable' area, women could feel unsafe. Lucille, a lone parent rehoused in a leafy suburb, felt disinclined to visit friends on her own at night unless she could afford a taxi back. It was so far out of town and public transport was bad. Similarly, another lone parent in the FSU study on a newly-built housing association estate felt extremely unsafe in the dark alleyways, whose design appeared attractive by day but threatening by night.

TRANSPORT

Transport was important for many people who lived on large out-of-town estates. However, even though most estates had a reasonably regular bus service into the city centre, at least during the day, there were still problems. Fares could be too expensive (see below) or buses difficult or impossible to use because of disability; women with several small children were effectively debarred from using them in practice.

Lack of transport seriously affected Lucille and the other lone parent mentioned above, rehoused on to smart new developments in relatively prosperous areas where most people had cars.

In 1989, Lucille tried to do an Employment Training course and stuck it out for three-and-a-half months. But because of lack of transport she had to give it up – she was paying £25 per week in taxi fares to attend the course. She also found it difficult to get into the town centre with her three young children and, as a result, was missing out on possible benefits. When interviewed late in October 1990, Lucille still had not managed to get down to the education offices to claim free school meals and a clothing grant for her second child who had started school in September.

For others, even relatively short journeys to see family were out of the question. One family who already had to forego 'luxuries' such as biscuits and a Sunday dinner had not seen the mother's parents for months, even though they lived less than an hour away by bus. They were simply unable to afford the bus fares.

SHOPPING

The availability of cheap local shops made a lot of difference to how people managed. Some, though not all, of the people in inner-city areas had the compensation of access to cheap markets, cost-cutting supermarkets and a variety of late-opening corner shops. One couple in Brixton were relatively lucky:

> They've got Kwiksave, Tesco's, we're going to have a big Argos . . . I've got loads of friends on stalls down in the market where I can get stuff cheap.

The range of shops was much more limited on the estates. In the

Bradford estate, the shopping facilities had at one time been regarded as adequate but were increasingly becoming run-down. The shopping precinct presented a bleak prospect with shops boarded-up or protected with wire mesh to prevent vandalism. The economic climate had added to the decline; at the time of interviewing the only launderette was about to be closed and replaced by a video shop.

Local shops on the estate were described generally as 'very expensive'. It was thought better to shop in the big stores in town, which were cheaper and offered greater choice. Similar issues came up on other estates. When people could, they travelled to cheaper shops, but often they lacked the money for fares, especially if they were having to budget from day to day for food (see Chapter 3).

For Asian families, 'tick' (credit) from the local Asian community shops often formed an important part of the budgeting arrangements. For some, local shopkeepers were the first point of call when the giro arrived – not to buy, but to pay off some or all of their accumulated debts. One family expressed this relationship eloquently:

> When the hand is empty, then if we need to get something desperately, say to eat, then I will get it on tick . . . but otherwise we just sit quietly . . .

As we have seen, by being locked into a relationship with local shops in this way (however useful a service this might be in the short-term), Asian families were trapping themselves into long-term financial difficulties and indebtedness just as severe and 'dependent' as those experienced by other families making use of the social fund. Borrowing from local shopkeepers became simply another expression of a vicious circle of debt.

7 Conclusion

We hope that the Government and Parliament will give high priority to a wide-ranging reform of social assistance. If nothing is done, things will not stand still. The supplementary benefits scheme will deteriorate as unemployment rises and the numbers depending on the scheme continue to grow, as cuts in local services impel people who might otherwise have been helped by education, housing and social service authorities to seek grants from us, and as the relationships of our service with other services become increasingly confused. If social security staff are reduced in numbers, things will get worse still. That is a sombre prospect. For this is not some residual corner of the 'welfare state'. It is the principal instrument for ensuring that nearly one in ten of the British people are lifted out of poverty and enabled to keep a foothold in the community.

(Annual Report of the Supplementary Benefits Commission,
1978, para 1.33)

He had never felt poor, and he had no power of imagining the part which the want of money plays in determining the actions of men.

Middlemarch, George Eliot

In Chapter 1, we outlined the tradition of research into poverty in this country. However, valuable though this tradition undoubtedly is, there is also a need for research 'from below', to complement it. It is important to listen directly to the people who are immediately affected by the social policies in question, and with the technology available to late twentieth century society there is no technical reason why we cannot do so. The problem of hearing 'the views of the poor' is not, in the last analysis, a technical one but a political one, a problem of acknowledging the importance of the perspective of those who experience poverty.

This book has been an attempt, albeit a limited one, to facilitate the process of hearing those views. We hope it will help politicians, policy-makers and commentators to be less dependent on their imagination when attempting to assess how social policies are experienced by those on the receiving end.

LIVING ON SOCIAL SECURITY

The findings reported in this book suggest that the forebodings of the Supplementary Benefits Commission were well-founded. Despite two wide-ranging reforms of social assistance (one implemented in 1980 and the other in 1988), the current system still fails, in many ways, to assist the very people it was set up to help. Indeed, the people we interviewed felt very much that this had been the case and described in detail the adverse effects the 1988 changes had had on them.

THE SOCIAL SECURITY CHANGES

The interviews highlighted a number of effects of recent social security policies:

- Most people interviewed felt that income support did not provide an adequate standard of living. Many felt worse off over the last few years and, in many cases, specifically cited the 1988 changes as being a main cause.
- It was usually impossible for claimants to budget effectively from week to week. This problem had grown worse since 1988, when they had had to start paying water rates and 20 per cent of the general rates/poll tax and had found that benefit increases did not adequately compensate for this. Money was often tight or ran out at the end of the week, leading to debt, deprivation and even shortage of food.
- Budgeting was made much harder by the removal of most lump-sum grants and the introduction of loans. Once again, benefit

levels did not take account of this change. Far from increasing independence and promoting budgeting skills, the removal of most grants was generally associated with increased debt, doing without essential items and/or a forced (and resented) dependence on help from family or friends.

- Families with children, people with disabilities and elderly people were all suffering. This indicated that the introduction of additional 'premiums' for groups with special expenses did not achieve its aim of targeting help on those seen by the government as most in need, although it did mean that claimants automatically received money for extra needs, instead of having to make a separate claim. It is of particular concern that health-related expenses were often not met, or met only with great difficulty.

- Although the 1988 changes were designed to make benefits simpler and easier to understand, people reported continuing difficulties in coping with social security administration, and in knowing what they were entitled to. For some, an internalised sense of stigma attached to being on benefit was exacerbated by stigmatising treatment from officialdom.

Since this research was carried out, there have been some minor improvements in the real level of benefit for some groups of income support claimants. However, these increases have not, in any way, been generous enough to contradict the overall conclusions of this book. The situations described here are so serious for many claimants that an extra pound or two a week does not make the necessary difference to raise their standard of living to an acceptable level.

INDIRECT EFFECTS OF POVERTY

The people we interviewed were affected by lack of money in many ways. They discussed their struggles to counteract the psychological pressures and stresses of poverty, and the difficulties these could produce in relationships with friends and within the family. They explained how a shortage of cash could curtail their participation in social and community activities.

Both studies highlighted the additional problems caused by poor housing and a run-down environment with a lack of local facilities (for example, cheap shops, good transport and play provision for children). These produced practical problems resulting in money worries, but also drastically affected people's quality of life. In addition, some lone parents felt strongly that lack of childcare facilities meant that they could not get into work and off benefit.

In summary, the accounts of living in poverty presented in this book bear witness to the continuing failure of social policies aimed at people in poverty. Above all, they present unequivocal evidence that the income support system is failing to meet the needs of the very people it was designed to help.

THE TWO STUDIES

The material presented in this book was drawn from two separate and independently organised research studies by Bradford University and Family Service Units (FSU), both carried out in 1989 and 1990. Both involved in-depth interviews with income support claimants, listening to how they viewed their situation, living on social security, in the context of the 1988 benefit changes. Although detailed numerical information was collected from the more structured parts of the interview schedules (eg, concerning levels of benefit received or claims made to the social fund), neither project aimed to interview a sample which would be fully representative of all income support claimants in a statistical sense, or to produce statistics from which general quantitative conclusions could be drawn. For information about published research that does do this, see the Bibliography. Rather, the studies used 'qualitative' research methods, tape-recording substantial interviews with relatively small numbers of people, hoping to provide more freedom for the interviewee to respond to open-ended questioning. Thus, more complex issues and processes were tackled, and claimants' own views on their experiences were heard, producing material of a kind which should complement the statistical data about poverty collected elsewhere. The value of qualitative research in providing insights into the experience of poverty, adding a solid dimension to the skeletons of statistical debate, has long been accepted by CPAG.

Wherever possible (eg, in relation to household benefit income), researchers checked the figures given by interviewees against relevant objective data (eg, prevailing benefit rates). Although the studies are relatively small-scale and do not claim to be statistically representative, many of our findings correspond with those of other researchers. In particular, we would point to studies by Berthoud (1984), Bradshaw and Holmes (1989), Craig and Glendinning (1990) and Ritchie (1990) (see Bibliography).

RACE AND POVERTY

Both projects were concerned about the little consideration given, in previous research on poverty and social security, to the experience of black people. As a result, over a third of the interviews in both studies were with claimants of Asian extraction (mostly Mirpuri Muslims from Pakistan), and were conducted in the language of their choice (usually Punjabi or Urdu). The material from these interviews is not intended to be presented as a picture of the experience of all claimants of Asian extraction, or even of all Pakistani Muslim claimants. In fact, there were some differences of emphasis between the interviewees in Bradford and those in the FSU study, reflecting different religious and cultural traditions. But, as very little research of this kind exists to date, it is hoped that it may describe some ways in which the social security system impacts on black people, highlighting issues which could be followed up in future research. For ease of reference in the text, these claimants are referred to as 'Asian' claimants (though most had British nationality).

The projects also wanted to consider the specific experience of claimants from other ethnic groups, including those for whom English is a first language. Indeed both projects originally set out to interview a group of Afro-Caribbean or Black British claimants as well as other Asians and White British. However, probably partly because of the way the researchers found the interviewees, this proved difficult to achieve. In the end, people of Black/Afro-Caribbean origin constituted only seven of the 45 FSU claimants (see below). An even smaller number (three) were interviewed in Bradford, again despite considerable efforts by the research team to locate suitable interviewees. This means that, although the experiences of some Black/Afro-Caribbean people are included in the research and add to the overall findings, there is not enough information to draw separate conclusions about them as a group, as has been done in a number of instances for Asian claimants.

SICKNESS AND DISABILITY

Neither study set out to look specifically at claimants with disabilities or who were sick. However, both found a high level of chronic ill-health and disability among the people interviewed – a finding reflected in other recent research on poverty (see Bibliography).

HOW THE STUDIES WERE ORGANISED

Both studies were concerned with people living on income support and did not, therefore, consider other groups of people often regarded as being in poverty (eg, those on low wages or those with long-term disabilities not on income support). There were also differences in the aims of these two studies and in how they were organised.

FAMILY SERVICE UNITS' STUDY

FSU is a long-established charity working with families and children in poor neighbourhoods through 22 local units in large towns in England and Scotland, and offering a range of social and community work services. FSU has always been committed to publishing research which demonstrates how government policies affect families using its services.

FSU set up the family poverty research project in 1989, to examine the experience of families with children living on income support. The FSU research project *only looked at claimants with children*, and everyone interviewed had had some contact with their local FSU. It considered, in detail, the financial positions of the claimants – eg, benefit received by each, whether they were in debt and how much for, what strategies they employed for budgeting, and the effects of benefit changes, including the introduction of the social fund. It also examined the social and emotional consequences of living on income support, focusing on the claimants' own perceptions and experiences. Each person was seen twice, with a year's interval between the interviews.

The 45 families were found by approaching people in touch with FSU services – eg, a child in the family attended a summer playscheme or, at the other extreme, a family who had used the local Unit and helped to run it for several years. A 'quota' sampling method was used, to gain lone parents and couples from Units in different parts of the country, from different ethnic groups, with varying numbers of children and on benefit for varying lengths of time. In the end, 26 lone parents and 19 couples were interviewed. In 1989, over a third (18) had four or more children and two-thirds (31) had been on benefit for three years or more. This preponderance of larger families and longer-term claimants probably reflects the make-up of people using FSU's services. Over half the families (27) lived in council accommodation, five were privately renting, five lived in trust/housing association property and eight were owner-occupiers. Again, the types of housing reflect the FSU catchment areas. Many FSUs serve large council estates, while nearly all the owner-occupiers we saw were Asian families using one FSU in a run-down inner-city area in a large Midlands town.

As already explained above, the research was intended to cover people from several ethnic groups but failed to find many people from Afro-Caribbean backgrounds. More success was had with Asian families because an Asian community worker in one Midlands FSU helped extensively. For this reason, most of the Asian families interviewed lived in that area and, except for three Sikh families from India, were all Muslims from Mirpur in Pakistan. The final sample included 16 Asian families, six of Black/Afro-Caribbean origin, 22 White British and one mixed race couple.

Both sets of interviews (in 1989 and 1990) were tape-recorded and transcribed verbatim. All but one of the Asian claimants were interviewed in their mother tongue of Punjabi or Urdu. (The findings from the first set of interviews alone have also been reported in *FSU Quarterly*, 'Do Families Benefit?', Issue No. 46, November 1990, and some of the implications for social policies are spelt out in a set of four policy pamphlets under the title 'Just About Surviving'; all are available from FSU Head Office.)

BRADFORD UNIVERSITY'S SOCIAL FUND RESEARCH PROJECT

The Bradford University social fund research project differed from the FSU research by *looking at the situation of single people, childless couples and pensioners as well as families with children*. It aimed to provide a qualitative complement to the quantitative research in progress under the auspices of the Social Security Research Consortium (see SSRC, 1991, in the Bibliography). Thus, it took account of the growing interest in the problem of unmet need, and the importance of looking at other strategies for budgeting used by low-income families. With this in mind, a number of extended interviews were conducted to explore claimants' experience of the social fund, both in relation to other financial strategies open to them for budgeting on benefit, and to their experience of the benefit system as a whole.

The research was carried out in two areas in Bradford. The first was a large council estate on the outskirts of the city, quite well-served by public transport but lacking good shops and other community facilities. It housed families with children and some pensioners, and was predominantly 'white'. The second area was an inner-city neighbourhood of old terraced housing, relatively well-served by public transport and shops. It contained a large and long-established Pakistani community, mostly owner-occupiers, and also a fairly transient population of single people. Several hostels for the homeless were in the area. Both areas had a long-standing and generally well-regarded community advice centre and the support of these centres was important in obtaining a demographic profile of the area which facilitated the process of 'screening' potential interviewees (found by door-knocking). It also gave valuable contacts in the community which encouraged co-operation with the research.

The Bradford researchers interviewed 91 people in all, between November 1989 and May 1990. As with the FSU study, it used a 'quota sample' approach, screening potential interviewees to obtain the groups we were looking for. Of the 91 claimants, about three-fifths (56) were white (all British except for one); just over a third (32) were Asian; and three were Black/Afro-Caribbean. All the interviews with the Asian families were conducted in their mother tongue of Urdu or Pakistani by Asian researchers.

We interviewed four types of claimant, using categories matching those of the DSS, in order to explore whether different groups experienced the benefit system in significantly different ways. A third (30) were couples with children, 22 were lone parents, 16 were pensioners and 23 were single or childless couples. As with the FSU study, one-third of the families with children had four or more children, with slightly more than half of the Asian families having a more complicated household structure involving older adult dependants or 'adult children' within the household. Six out of ten two-parent families, and nine out of ten lone-parent families, had been on benefit for three years or more. Less than one-third of those without children had been on benefit this long. Six out of ten pensioners had been on retirement-related benefits for ten years or more.

Housing tenure was seen as a significant but subsidiary factor in canvassing for the quotas and, in practice, we could not maintain a balance between housing tenures or respondents as well as between claimant type and ethnicity. Virtually all of the interviews conducted on the peripheral estate were with council tenants; of those in the inner-city area, just over half were owner-occupiers and the rest mainly private tenants.

As with the FSU study, the interviews were lengthy (averaging more than an hour) and were tape-recorded and transcribed onto schedules for the purpose of analysis. The interviews covered some of the same ground as the FSU study, looking at claimants' financial circumstances, debts, budgeting strategies, the effects of shortage of money on family and social relationships, and how claimants felt about living on social security and dealing with the benefit authorities. But the Bradford research was particularly interested in assessing claimants' experiences of the social fund.

Claimants were asked specifically which of the following items they had, and what condition they were in. Claimants were told to include items not owned but which they were able to use:

- Washing machine
- Vacuum cleaner
- Fridge
- Freezer

- Cooker
- Iron
- B/W TV
- Colour TV

- Electric Kettle
- Telephone
- Car
- Video

They were also asked which of the of the following 'goods' or 'services' they possessed. If they did not have a particular item, claimants were asked if this was because they couldn't afford it:

- A holiday away for a week a year (for Asian families: a trip to visit relatives in another town once a year).
- Two pairs of all-weather shoes for everyone in the household.
- A night out once a fortnight.
- Friends/family round for a meal once a week.
- Children's friends round for tea/snack once a fortnight.
- A 'best' outfit of clothes for special events (a party; Eid etc).
- Two satisfactory hot meals a day.
- Sweets and fruit for children twice a week.
- A selection of toys at home for children to play with.

The interview schedule was developed with reference to those used in earlier studies of family poverty and reported in Mack and Lansley (1984), Noble et al (1987), Bradshaw and Holmes (1989) and Craig and Glendinning (1990) – see Bibliography. Several questions were altered or offered in alternative formulations to take account of the ethnic diversity of the respondents. The schedule was piloted in two areas similar to those in which the final study was conducted.

Copies of the interview schedules used can be obtained from FSU head office or from Gary Craig (via Bradford University) as appropriate.

BIBLIOGRAPHY

RECENT STUDIES AND RESEARCH INTO FAMILY POVERTY

(Place of publication is London unless otherwise stated)

The reports listed chronologically below are those of greatest relevance to this book. They include primary and secondary research studies of family poverty defined in its widest sense, concerned with the description of, and not solely with, definitions or the measurement of, poverty.

Lister, R and Emmett, T (1976), *Under the safety net*, CPAG
Reviews evidence relating to the use of Section 1 (1963 Children and Young Person's Act) money for purposes which inappropriately 'provide a safety net for poor families who are refused help by the Supplementary Benefits Commission under its powers to provide lump-sum grants and emergency payments', and shows that the pressures on local social services departments have been exacerbated by the closure of many local DSS offices.

Clark, M (1978), 'The unemployed on supplementary benefit', *Journal of Social Policy*, Vol 7, Pt 4, Cambridge, pp385-410
Based on a 'national survey of 1535 unemployed men on supplementary benefit in 1974'. Effect of low incomes was the inability to accumulate savings, clothing or household equipment to cushion them in unemployment. Large unemployed families had the greatest difficulty in managing.

Townsend, P (1979), *Poverty in the United Kingdom*, Penguin, Harmondsworth
Findings from a comprehensive national survey of 2,000 households. Case material used to illustrate multi-dimensional nature of poverty. Chief conclusion is that poverty 'is more extensive than is generally or officially believed . . . (it) is a national phenomenon which is structurally pervasive and of major dimensions.'

Burghes, L (1980), *Living from hand to mouth*, FSU/CPAG
Study of 65 families living on supplementary benefit. Almost all families had to borrow to make ends meet and were in debt as a result.

Durward, Lyn (1981), *That's the way the money goes*, Disability Alliance
Small study identifying twelve areas in which people with disabilities might bear additional costs. 'There was ample evidence to suggest tht people with disabilities do not simply have to forego holidays and leisure activities because of the costs involved; significant numbers sometimes go without meals, without heating, without adequate clothing, because their incomes are insufficient to meet their needs.'

Piachaud, D (1981), *Children and poverty,* **CPAG**
Updating of earlier study (*The Cost of A Child,* CPAG, 1979). The 1981 study concluded that 'the level of provision for children in families dependent on supplementary benefit is substantially below the minimum needed to meet the costs of children [and] the extent of poverty amongst children has been substantially under-estimated.'

Ashley, P (1983), *The money problems of the poor: a literature review,* **Heinemann**
Part of a larger programme of research into 'Transmitted Deprivation'. Observes that 'low income creates vulnerability . . . [and] . . . of those receiving supplementary benefit, the unemployed have the lowest long-term incomes relative to requirements.'

Bradshaw, J, Cooke, K and Godfrey, G (1983), 'The impact of unemployment on the living standards of families', *Journal of Social Policy,* **Vol 12, Pt 4, Cambridge, pp433-452**
Analysis of data from the Family Finances Survey. 'The living standards of the long-term unemployed are lower than those in short-term unemployment and . . . the living standards of both are below those of the poorest families in work.' (See also: Hakim, C. [1982], 'The Social Consequences of High Unemployment', *Journal of Social Policy,* Vol 11, Pt 4, Cambridge.)

FSU (1983), *Social insecurity,* **Family Service Units**
Analysis of views and experience of local Family Service Units relating to the administration of supplementary benefits. 'The scale rates are inadequate to maintain a normal social existence . . . the system is still so complex that few claimants can know in detail which benefits they are entitled to . . . A significant proportion of all supplementary benefit claimants receive poor standards of service.'

Roll, J (1983), *Worse off on the dole,* **mimeo, CPAG**
Review of evidence as to how many people are better off financially out of work. Only three per cent of white unemployed men and five per cent of minority group men were receiving more in benefit than they were from their previous earnings.

Allbeson, J and Smith, R (1984), *We don't give clothing grants any more,* **The 1980 Supplementary Benefit Scheme, CPAG**
Evaluation of 1980 social security reforms, especially new single payment arrangements. 'Complication and low take-up are . . . unavoidable problems of the use of a mass means-tested scheme as the source of benefit of last resort.' The 1980 scheme brought 'an unacknowledged cut in claimants' entitlements by way of the reduction in clothing grants. This particularly affected families with children.' Charities and local authorities 'increasingly fulfilling the role of ultimate source of help'.

Berthoud, R (1984), *The reform of supplementary benefit,* **Policy Studies Institute**
Comprehensive large-scale investigation into the 1980 supplementary benefit reforms. Underclaiming of single payments widespread; supplementary benefit levels viewed by staff and claimants as inadequate, especially for families with children; introduction of regulations had little effect on judgement or discretion exercised by supplementary benefit officers. Observations in local offices identified significant racism.

Brown, Colin (1984), *Black and white Britain,* **Gower/Policy Studies Institute**
Survey into circumstances of British black population. Unemployment rates are higher and have been growing at a much faster rate for Asian and West Indian men and women than for white workers, and were particularly high for young black people.

Cooke, K and Baldwin, S (1984), *How much is enough?,* **Family Policy Studies Centre**
Reviews range of evidence about adequacy of supplementary benefit scale rates. Amongst unemployed families, 56 per cent borrowed money for food, 35 per cent for clothes or shoes, 34 per cent for heating and fuel. Fifty-one per cent of families of unemployed men had children with second-hand shoes. Current benefit levels are result of piecemeal political decision-making and 'clearly defined budgetary standards should be adopted'.

Fagin, L and Little, M (1984), *The forsaken families,* **Penguin, Harmondsworth**
Interviews with a small sub-sample of families drawn from the 1978 DHSS national cohort study of the unemployed. Evidence strongly suggests association between ill-health and unemployment.

Mack, J and Lansley, S (1984), *Poor Britain,* **Allen and Unwin**
Study found general agreement about what constituted a minimum standard of living. Being in poverty defined as 'a situation in which people had to live without the things which society as a whole regarded as necessities'. One in seven of the population (ie over 7 million people) lacked three or more necessities. Study repeated with modifications in 1990 (*Breadline Britain in the 1990s,* Harper Collins, 1992).

Moylan, S et al (1984), *For richer or poorer?,* **DHSS cohort study of unemployed men, Research Report No 11, DHSS/HMSO**
Large-scale survey of incomes of men 'who become unemployed, their financial incentives to work and their experience of employment and unemployment'. Men's earnings in work had been far below the national average – half had gross earnings in the bottom fifth of the income distribution. Few men started unemployment with substantial savings, half had none at all. Less than one-fifth of those eligible for FIS actually received it.

Bourne, J (1985), 'Counting the cost', *New Society*, **Sept 6, pp350-351**
Analysis of adequacy of supplementary benefit rates for under-25s. Demonstrates that further reduction in benefits 'risks infringing "the basic responsibility of any government" – namely that everyone should get an income adequate to sustain themselves' (see also: Craig, G. [1991], *Fit for nothing?*, Children's Society/COYPSS).

Howe, LEA (1985), 'The "deserving" and the "undeserving": practice in an urban local social security office', *Journal of Social Policy*, **Vol 14, Pt 1, Cambridge, pp49-72**
Based on 'three months' research in an inner city social security office in Northern Ireland in 1982'. Legal basis of the scheme had little impact on welfare promotion. Workloads and staffing levels create further difficulties for staff and claimants and 'local practice exhibits a significant moralist practice' (see also Howe, LEA [1990]) *Being unemployed in Northern Ireland*, Cambridge University Press, Cambridge).

Gordon, P and Newnham, A (1985), *Passport to benefits?: racism in social security*, **CPAG/Runnymede Trust**
Examination of ways in which racism operates within social security system. Includes analysis of links between social security administration and operation of immigration laws, and description of means by which claimants are treated as second-class citizens as result of institutional racism and ethnocentricity. (See also: NACAB, [1991], *Barriers to benefit*, National Association of Citizens' Advice Bureaux.)

Golding, P (ed), (1986), *Excluding the poor*, **CPAG**
'Poverty is not only a matter of a lack of money. It also creates a barrier preventing millions of people from participating fully in society . . . ' Shows 'how low income families are excluded from leisure pursuits, political life, various financial institutions and from the new entertainment and communication technologies'. (See also: Lister, R. [1990], *The exclusive society: Citizenship and the poor*, CPAG.)

Stewart, G with Stewart, J (1986), *Boundary changes: social work and social security*, **CPAG/BASW**
Review of impact of 'shifting boundaries' between social services provision and social security provision.

Bradshaw, J R and Morgan, J (1987), 'Budgeting on benefit', *New Society*, **March 6, pp17-19**
Draws on earlier work by Piachaud but employs a basket of goods or 'budget standard' method 'constrained by what people on supplementary benefit on average actually spend their money on'. Analysis reveals a pattern of living which is 'drab, limited and inflexible'.

Brannen, J and Wilson, G (1987), *Give and take in families***, Studies in resource distribution, Allen and Unwin**
'The focus of this book is the distribution of material resources, notably money, work, care and food, within and between households.' Concludes that 'access to resources within households is structured by . . . power relationships which are themselves structured by gender, class and race.'

Disability Alliance (1987), *Poverty and disability***, Disability Alliance**
Case for a comprehensive disability income scheme is reviewed. Almost 60 per cent of disabled population living in or on the margins of poverty (more than twice the rate in the population at large) and as many as 50 per cent of all disabled people in some studies not claiming full entitlement to benefits.

Glendinning, C and Millar, J (eds), (1987), *Women and poverty***, Wheatsheaf, Brighton**
A review of position of women and poverty in the UK. Roots of women's poverty clearly embedded in sexual division of labour which places women in secondary and marginal position. Out of the labour market, women are similarly disadvantaged. 'The ideology of dependency essentially legitimates women's poverty . . . women's assumed and actual dependence on men is in fact the major cause of their poverty.'

Noble, M *et al* **(1987),** *The other Oxford***, University of Oxford, Oxford**
Report of a survey of 259 low-income households in Oxford. Findings show that 'current benefit levels are not adequate for many households'; families with children are under greatest financial pressure; and at this level of income there is 'little margin for error and little scope for choice'. Outlines coping strategies including reductions in expenditure, going into debt and doing without. The 'effects of the benefit changes in April 1988 would have meant many more losers than gainers among the study households.'

Cohen, R and Tarpey, M (eds) (1988), *Single payments: the disappearing safety net***, CPAG Ltd**
Review of evidence from a range of organisations about the impact of the cuts in single payment entitlements in 1986. Charities and local authorities have to fill gaps created by cuts and three groups have been particularly hard hit: young single people, lone parents and unemployed families.

McKenna, S and Gurney, J (1988), *In hock to the state***, Leicester CPAG, Leicester**
Study of the early months of the social fund in Leicestershire. Found low levels of knowledge and understanding of fund, and wide incidence of unmet need. 'For many claimants, the social fund heralds the disappearance of the safety net, and the prospect of levels of hardship unknown in recent times.'

Bradshaw, J R and Holmes, H (1989), *Living on the edge***, Tyneside CPAG, Tyneside**
Study of 67 long-term unemployed families on supplementary benefit. Families on supplementary benefit spent half as much as the average person on food, went without items of clothing, cut down on heating, and had many household goods in bad condition. Families were socially isolated and worried about impact of poverty on their children. Picture is 'one of constant restriction in almost every aspect of people's activities'.

Berthoud, R (1989), *Credit, debt and poverty***, SSAC Research Paper, No 1, SSAC/HMSO**
More than half unemployed families with children in debt; loans not acceptable as way of meeting their lump sum needs; money advice offered by social fund officers may lead to further confusion between financial and welfare problems; and falling into debt is one common way for claimants to manage meeting needs on inadequate income (see also: Parker, G. [1990] *Getting and Spending,* Avebury, Aldershot; Berthoud, R and Kempson, E [1992], *Credit and debt*, PSI, London).

Craig, G (ed), (1989), *Your flexible friend?***, Association of Metropolitan Authorities/Social Security Consortium**
Review of experience of voluntary agencies and charities in relation to the social fund. Concludes that social fund is not achieving its stated objective of 'targeting help on those in greatest need' and that it is inconsistent and unfair.

Evason, E, Allamby, L and Woods, R (1989), *The deserving and undeserving poor***, CPAG Northern Ireland, Derry**
A small-scale study of the social fund in Northern Ireland. Found that fund had 'a strong impact on the Society of St Vincent de Paul', the major grant-giving charity in the province, and that its role had been restructured away from an all-round advice agency to one dispensing aid to those in need. (See also: Evason, E. [1986] *On the edge: poverty and unemployment in Northern Ireland*, CPAG.)

McLaughlin, E *et al* **(1989),** *Work and welfare benefits***, Avebury, Aldershot**
Study based on interviews with 50 families in West Yorkshire and Northern Ireland; examines effectiveness of low level unemployment benefits and means-tested wages supplements in getting people back to work. Demonstrates that current income support policy for unemployed and low paid people is unlikely to succeed while resting on certain assumptions about financial incentives. 'Meeting basic household needs was the main consideration the family took into account when thinking about wages.'

Millar, J (1989), *Poverty and the lone parent family*, **Avebury, Aldershot**
An analysis of living standards of lone parents in Britain. Solutions to the poverty of lone parent families 'may have to mean fairly radical changes to our views of the duties and obligations of parents and the state towards children' (see also: Bradshaw, J and Millar, J [1991] *Lone parent families in the UK*, DSS/HMSO).

Townsend, P and Gordon, D (1989), *What is enough?*, **Memorandum of Evidence to House of Commons Social Services Committee, Inquiry into Minimum Income, August, University of Bristol, Bristol**
'New evidence, drawn principally from a survey in Greater London in 1985-6, which shows that levels of means-tested assistance in Britain have been, and are, substantially lower than levels of income required to surmount poverty.'

Becker, S and Silburn, R (1990), *The new poor clients*, **Nottingham University Benefits Research Unit/Community Care, Surrey**
Final report of BRU monitoring of social fund, which covered 27 local authorities in Great Britain. Builds on earlier report (*Poor clients*, Becker, S and McPherson, S, 1986, BRU) examining relationship between social work, poverty and social security. Concludes that 'social services departments have been affected by the introduction of the social fund but not perhaps as dramatically or as destructively as was feared.'

Bradshaw, J (1990), *Child poverty and deprivation in the UK*, **National Children's Bureau**
Part of international study by UNICEF looking at child poverty and deprivation in eight major industrialised countries.

Craig, G and Glendinning, C (1990), *Missing the target*, **Barnardo's, Barkingside**
Report on the impact of the 1988 social security changes on families using Barnardo's services. Concludes that most families had lost as a result of changes and were facing mounting debts and arrears. Poverty 'has a damaging and limiting effect on family life' and women were bearing the main burden (see also: Craig, G. and Glendinning, C. [1990] 'Parenting in Poverty', *Community Care*, March 15; Glendinning, C. and Craig, G. [1990], 'The Trickle Away Effect', *Community Care*, March 22.)

NACAB (1990), *Hard times for social fund applicants*, **National Association of Citizens' Advice Bureaux**
Second survey of claimants' experience of the social fund, based on data collected by local CABx. Clients reluctant to take out loans; unmet need widely identified and applicants for whom English is not a first language

were additionally disadvantaged. (See also: Clark, A. [1989] *After the social fund*, Citizens Advice Scotland.)

Oppenheim, C (1990), *Poverty: the facts*, CPAG Ltd

Comprehensive review of data and research evidence relating to the definition, causes and consequences of poverty in the UK. 'Poverty multiplied more rapidly (in the UK) between 1975 and 1985 than in any other country in the European Community.' 'Such poverty is not random but shaped by class, by gender and by race.'

Ritchie, J (1990), *Thirty families: their living standards in unemployment*, DSS

Families felt that standard of living they had in unemployment was lower than when they had been employed. Many families described what they saw as a continuing decline, at least for the first two or three years of unemployment until they hit 'rock bottom.'

Social Services Committee (1990), *Low income statistics*, HC 376, House of Commons

Based on analyses undertaken by the Institute for Fiscal Studies. Official claims that the lowest 10 per cent in terms of income had larger real increases in income (after housing costs) compared with other groups were considerably overstated as result of mistakes in DSS calculations. 'Far from this group experiencing the largest percentage increase in living standards, they have now been found to have had an increase over the period 1981/5 of only half the average increase experienced by the total population' (see also: DHSS [1988] *Households below average income*, 1981/5, HMSO; Townsend, P. [1991] *The poor get poorer*, University of Bristol.)

Morris, L, with Llewellyn, T (1991), *Social security provision for the unemployed*, SSAC/HMSO

Detailed review of benefits provision for unemployed people, largely focusing on experience of UK but with reference to situation in four other states.

Social Security Research Consortium (1991), *Cash limited: limited cash?*, Association of County Councils/Association of Metropolitan Authorities

Report drawing together findings from main survey of the SSRC local authority social services department monitoring, together with other elements of SSRC work including advice centre monitoring in five conurbations.